sew me!

sewing basics

sewing basics

Simple Techniques and Projects for First-Time Sewers

Choly Knight

an Imprint of Fox Chapel Publishing
www.d-originals.com

ACQUISITION EDITOR
Peg Couch

COPY EDITOR
Colleen Dorsey

COVER AND PAGE DESIGNER
Lindsay Hess

COVER AND PROJECT PHOTOGRAPHER
Scott Kriner

EDITOR
Katie Weeber

LAYOUT DESIGNER
Maura J. Zimmer

STEP-BY-STEP PHOTOGRAPHER
Matthew McClure

ISBN 978-1-57421-423-9

Library of Congress Cataloging-in-Publication Data

Knight, Choly.
  Sew me! sewing basics / Choly Knight.
    pages cm
  Includes index.
  ISBN 978-1-57421-423-9
  1. Machine sewing. I. Title.
  TT713.K58 2013
  646.2'044--dc23
                    2013001609

© 2013 by Choly Knight and Design Originals, www.d-originals.com, an imprint of Fox Chapel Publishing, 800-457-9112,
1970 Broad Street, East Petersburg, PA 17520.

Printed in China
First printing

About the Author

Choly Knight is from Orlando, Florida, and is the author of *Sew Kawaii!*, *Sew Baby*, and *Sewing Stylish Handbags*. She has been crafting for as long as she can remember, and has drawn, painted, sculpted, and stitched everything in sight. She began sewing clothing in 1997 and has yet to put her sewing machine away. After studying studio art and earning a BA in English, she now enjoys trying to find numerous different ways to combine her passions for writing, fine art, and craft art. She created all of the designs, projects, and patterns appearing in this book. She focuses on handcrafted clothing, accessories, and other creations inspired by Japanese art, anime, and style, and specializes in cosplay (costume play) hats and hoodies. You can find out more about her and her work on her website: *www.cholyknight.com*.

Author Choly Knight

Contents

Build Your Skills One Project at a Time!

This book is perfect for first-time sewers, as it allows you to build your skills through practical application. As a first step, read the Getting Started chapter (page 12) to get a handle on the types of tools and materials you'll be working with and familiarize yourself with your sewing machine. Then the fun begins! In each of the following chapters, you will learn a series of techniques. Each technique is followed by a project that incorporates the technique you just learned, giving you the chance to put your newfound knowledge to use right away. The projects are fun, simple, and easily personalized to your own taste, so you'll have every incentive to jump right in and start sewing. Use these pages as a checklist to track your progress!

48 YOUR FIRST SEAM   **58** HAND SEWING   **64** APPLIQUÉ

57 DEALING WITH MISTAKES

70 SEWING CURVES   **80** INTERFACING   **85** GATHERING FABRIC

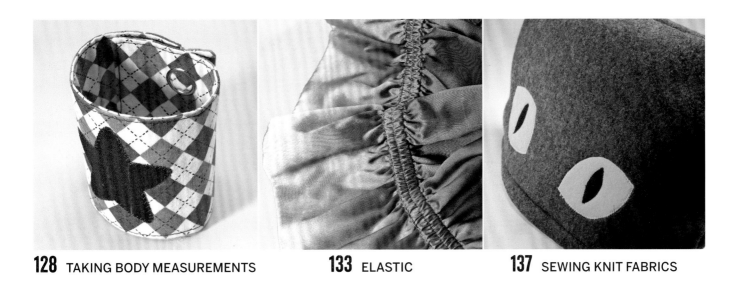

Introduction

If you've picked up this book, then something about sewing has gotten you excited. Maybe you're entranced by the idea of making designer clothes worthy of the most elite runways. Or perhaps you have an empty apartment that screams for soft furnishings and bright colors. Maybe you've found yourself the owner of a new sewing machine and want to find out what makes it tick. Or it could be that you yearn for that feeling of working with your own two hands, whether it's for yourself, friends, or those closest to you. No matter what your reasons, you have curiosity, and this book will help you fulfill that curiosity.

Even though I've been a crafty little thing since childhood, it wasn't until I was twelve years old that the sewing bug caught up with me. When I was younger I much preferred the beautiful palette of colors in my paint kit to my mother's old leather sewing kit—a mess of tangled thread, strange metal parts, and

fabric patches in dull, neutral colors. While I sculpted clay and made jewelry, I avoided my mother's sewing machine, knowing that I would likely break it as soon as I touched it.

As curious as you might be to try your hand at sewing, it can still be intimidating to lug out a (possibly brand new) machine, invest in fabric and supplies, clear your weekend, and hope that you can make the gamble worthwhile. But I can tell you now that sewing doesn't need to be that way. What finally brought me over to sewing was my first Home Economics class in middle school. The class project was a simple drawstring backpack, but seeing how a few simple yards of cotton could be transformed into a useful item made me realize the limitless possibilities sewing had. The machine, shears, and needles were only tools—I just had to find out what made them tick and then they were mine to control.

I asked the teacher if I could spend my extra class time adding pockets and zippers to my bag. Of course she kindly turned me down, saying "They're a bit difficult" and "Maybe next semester." But that didn't keep me from working on the bag as soon as I got home. I knew deep down the only thing holding me back was how much I could absorb.

Learning more from there was still a bit of an uphill battle. Other sewers I knew had only the most basic skills, and I found how-to sewing books difficult to get through. I felt they read more like encyclopedias. I understood the idea of making a welt pocket, but why would I want one? What was it best suited for? Did it always have to go on a mustard-colored pants suit? (Did I mention most of my how-to books were from thrift stores and old libraries?) The endless list of skill after skill just sat as a dead weight on my brain. With no practical application or explanation, I didn't know where to go with the information.

In this book, I've done away with the encyclopedia format to develop projects and techniques that you can really use. From the very beginning I'll show you how to pick out and take care of your sewing machine, and along the way, you'll learn all you need to know to

Once I figured out all that I could do with sewing, I didn't want to stop. I love creating my own custom designs that suit my taste and personality!

make projects that are not only useful, but stunning to boot! Instead of an encyclopedia list of technique after technique, I'll break each skill down so you understand its strengths and purpose, as well as how to implement it. Then you'll be able to try it out on a load of wonderful projects—some that only take a few minutes.

With all of this in hand, you'll find that learning to sew doesn't have to be scary, restricting, or expensive. You'll learn how your tools work so you are in control,

you'll learn the whys and hows of techniques so you can apply them anywhere, and you'll see just how creative sewing can be. There will be mistakes, and there will be headaches, but you'll see at most it will result in some stitches to rip or a bit of fabric wasted. No amount of frustration can compare with the feeling of creating your own one-of-a-kind sewn project, and this book will help take you on that fabulous journey!

Choly Kight

Sink Your Teeth In:
Getting Started

If you've never picked up a needle before, this is definitely where to begin. In this starting section, you'll be guided through how to pick out a sewing machine, choose fabrics and supplies, and how to follow a project. Don't be afraid of getting overwhelmed, as everything is taken step by step and you'll learn more as you go. Only the most basic requirements to get started are listed here, so there's nothing stopping you from diving right in!

Why Sew?
Attitudes Behind Sewing

People often ask me, why go through the trouble of sewing when extremely cheap clothing can be found just about anywhere? It's true, the cheapest clothing on the market can't compare with the cost of sewing for yourself, but there are lots of other reasons to sew beyond that.

Creative expression: You really can't beat the feeling of getting to make something from nothing—taking plain fabric and turning it into something useful and beautiful with just your two hands and a sewing machine. With enough projects, you'll begin to see raw materials in a whole new light. An old button-down shirt can become a new dress; old scraps of paper can be sewn into a notebook. Nothing you purchase can compare with that knowledge.

Frugality: Sure, sewing for yourself isn't nearly as cheap as bargain-basement wares, but suppose you want something more high-end? A fancy dress or a silky soft duvet cover? With the right shopping around you can easily spend less than half on fabric than what you would spend on the finished product at a department store. And you know what you'll make will last much longer with higher-quality materials and construction. The cost of tools and notions adds up at first, but if you keep sewing, then investment in quality tools will save you more and more money.

Individuality: Perhaps my personal favorite reason for sewing is complete control and individuality. I'm the kind of girl that knows exactly what she wants and won't settle for less. As artsy as I tend to be, I'm always disappointed by the selection of goods at retail stores. Sewing is how I know I can get exactly what I want—that I can wear the exact dress I imagined, or decorate my house with the exact colors that cheer me up the most. There's the added bonus that no one will have things quite like yours and you've probably accomplished it for less money!

The Beginning of a Beautiful Friendship:
Buying a Sewing Machine

If you are brand new to sewing, you may find yourself anxiously venturing to buy a new machine or find a hand-me-down. It doesn't have to be a stressful experience so long as you know what you are looking for. Reliable machines for first-time sewers can be acquired in a number of ways. One way to narrow down your choices is to decide what you hope to get out of your new machine.

YOUR SEWING STYLE: WHAT KIND OF SEWER ARE YOU?

First, consider just what kind of sewer are you? Even if you haven't picked up a needle and thread, think about how these personality types apply to other things you've created (especially if you're an artist or crafter!).

The Industrialist

You enjoy creating because it lets you work with your hands. You like taking raw materials and turning them into something useful, even if it takes considerable time and concentration. You usually care less what happens with your finished product because the process and being in control is what really drives you.

Your machine: Your best mate is likely a basic and dependable mechanical machine. Avoid models with computerized parts that will give you less control. A mechanical model gives you complete power over what happens, like an old faithful truck.

The Industrialist: You like to get down and dirty with your machine—fancy bells and whistles would only stand in your way.

The Fashionista

The end result is what gets you motivated for a project. The sooner you can get to wearing and showing off your new design the better. You particularly agree with the idea of form over function and don't worry so much over details as much as whether the end result looks good.

Your machine: A beginner's computerized machine will likely make you happiest. Even the more simple models have special features that take care of tedious tasks like threading the needle or reminding you to lower your presser foot, not to mention the oodles of decorative stitches for getting dazzling looks in a flash. Computerized versions might end up being more expensive, so a mechanical model is also fine, as long as you find the right features.

The Fashionista: You hate getting bogged down by tedious details and would rather be flaunting your project than fussing with it.

The Improviser

You are a true left-brain thinker and tend to make up rules as you go along. Your motivation for your project is getting to express yourself from start to finish. You might end up with some peculiar and strange creations, but you love them all the same.

Your machine: You will likely enjoy a hand-me-down or secondhand machine. Older machines tend to be more reliable (and cheaper!), but inevitably come with kinks or eccentricities. Your inventive nature will surely find ways to work around any quirks and become best friends with your machine.

The Improviser: You find a way to work under any condition because every setback just fuels your creativity.

STILL NOT SURE?

If your creative personality is not so hard and fast (whose is, really?), consider these sewing features that come with machines. Just like with a car, some features are truly crucial, others depend on your tastes, and still others are excessive and not worth the extra cost. Keep in mind that having additional features is not a problem, because you don't have to use them. Just don't let them force you into spending lots more money than you planned.

☐ **Zigzag stitches:** Nearly everything on this planet can be sewn with straight and zigzag stitches alone. There's no sense in messing with a good thing.

☐ **Specialty stitches:** If you only plan to do basic sewing, a straight and zigzag stitch can do it all for you. If you're a little more serious about sewing, additional utilitarian stitches like a blind hemstitch, overlock stitch, featherstitch, or stretch stitch will be of use to you as you learn more.

☐ **Decorative stitches:** These are a big selling point with a lot of machines. Simple circles and diamonds can be found on lower-end machines, and even flowers and animals can be found on expensive ones. Keep in mind that while decorative stitches look tempting, when they're sewn they're only about ¼" (0.5cm) wide, so you can barely see them from far away. Don't get overexcited about machines that offer hundreds of stitches if you plan to make projects that will barely show your embellishments. There are plenty of other ways to embellish your projects that make a much bigger impact.

☐ **Adjustable stitch length/width:** Some very basic machines only allow limited settings for stitch width and length. When it's adjustable, you have much more control over the stitches you're creating.

☐ **Free arm sewing:** This allows the bed of the machine to be removed or lowered so only a skinny arm is free for sewing tubes like sleeves and pant legs. This is standard on most modern machines, but it's helpful to check for it.

☐ **Metal vs. plastic parts:** Most modern machines come with plastic parts inside, such as for the bobbin and bobbin casing. These can melt and break more often than their older, metal ancestors. So if you can find a metal machine, really consider getting it!

☐ **Buttonhole stitch:** Buttonholes can be done freehand, but it's rarely worth the extra effort. A buttonhole stitch can make things much simpler. One-step and four-step varieties are the norm, and what works best for you can depend on your sewing personality. See the sewing buttons feature (page 106) and the chart at the right to make your decision.

☐ **Easy threading:** Threading a machine properly can take a little practice. Some modern models simplify the process by adding arrows and indicators. If you only plan to sew once in a great while, this can make things easier than sitting down with your manual every time you want to sew.

☐ **Presser foot pressure:** Some machines have a gauge that allows you to control how hard the presser foot presses on your fabric. You'll find it's helpful if you are finicky about results and getting serious about sewing.

☐ **Easy install presser feet/needles:** Most presser feet and needles require screws for installation, but some fancier versions offer easy ways to install these parts. They're not as secure as screws, but definitely more convenient.

☐ **Additional presser feet:** Keep an eye out for buttonhole presser feet, zipper feet, and blind hem presser feet if you see lots of clothes in your future. Anything extra isn't really necessary for a beginner.

☐ **Needle up/down button:** This feature allows you to hit one button to lift or lower the needle. Some prefer it, but I think it bumps up the overall price of the machine too much for something so simple.

☐ **Adjustable feed dogs:** This allows the feed dogs of the machine to be lowered so you can move the fabric freely yourself. This feature is mostly necessary for those who are serious about quilt making. Improvisers might like the option for freehand sewing.

☐ **Digital screens:** When you start encountering machines with big digital screens, it usually means you've ventured too far and are into luxury machine territory. Looking at any machine beyond this is sure to give you sticker shock.

	The Industrialist	The Fashionista	The Improviser
Zigzag stitches	✓	✓	✓
Specialty stitches	✓	✓	
Decorative stitches		✓	✓
Adjustable stitch length/width	✓		✓
Free arm sewing	✓	✓	✓
Metal parts	✓	✓	✓
Buttonhole stitch (1-step)		✓	
Buttonhole stitch (4-step)	✓		✓
Easy threading		✓	
Presser foot pressure	✓		
Easy install presser feet/needles		✓	
Additional presser feet	✓	✓	
Needle up/down button		✓	
Adjustable feed dogs			✓
Digital screens			

TAKING THE PLUNGE: MAKING THE PURCHASE

When you've finally decided on the features you want, the best thing to do is search your nearest sewing machine dealer so you can test machines yourself. They often service the machines at the same location, which makes dealing with tuning up a snap. Like with any dealership, make sure you know exactly what features you want and don't want so you don't end up spending more than you can handle.

You might notice some extremely expensive machines for embroidery and quilting with prices that easily reach thousands of dollars. Don't let them give you sticker shock! These machines are heavily computerized and are for serious hobbyists who want every convenience a machine can give. A very reliable and hardworking machine can usually be purchased for about $100, so don't let any errant high price tags scare you away.

Your next best bet after a dedicated sewing machine dealer is to purchase from your neighborhood craft store, as they might also let you test your machine before buying. You may also get a decent warranty on the machine so you can handle any issues as you get to know it.

Failing that, you can also get secondhand machines from friends, family, and thrift stores. You can check firsthand to see if most of the parts are moving and working. However, there's a good chance the machine will need to be tuned up before you get started, so try to get that done before taking on any serious projects to avoid a headache later. You might end up with an odd grab bag of features, but if you're the improvisational type, you'll enjoy the adventure.

Lastly, if no other option is available, buying online also works. It's risky because you can't try the machine beforehand, but finding listings for machines with lots of reliable reviews helps, especially if the machine offers a warranty to back up your purchase. While it's not a 100 percent guaranteed method, it's still possible to find a darn good machine online, and if you do run into problems, you might be able to work out the kinks with help from this book!

The chart on page 17 will give you a general idea of what sort of features to look for depending on your sewing personality. You might not be able to find every feature you want in a machine, but hopefully now you have a better idea of what's important to look for.

The Sewer's Palette: Fabrics

If you've been drawn to sewing because of the glamour, it's a good chance fabric is what first caught your eye. With a little bit of knowledge going in, the fabric store can feel less overwhelming and more like an adventurous hunt. Picking the right fabric can mean the difference between a project you'll want to keep forever and one that might turn you off to sewing. Here I'll break down all you need to know about finding and buying fabric so you're sure to be happy with your purchase.

The best way to categorize fabrics so you make the right choice is to divide them between fabrics that stretch and fabrics that don't. These are called wovens and knits. Beyond that, they are broken down by thickness or weight. If you learn to see fabric in this way, you can be sure to get the best fabric for the job. See page 24 for a handy chart listing the best uses for each different type of fabric.

WOVEN FABRICS

Woven fabrics are the kind that should come to mind when you think of your favorite button-down shirt, a sturdy tote bag, or a fancy pair of slacks. These fabrics are made by weaving threads together, just like basket pieces, to form the fabric. They can be made from synthetic or natural fibers and range from large weaves like burlap to delicate weaves like fine silk.

Lightweight wovens

Lightweight woven fabrics encompass some very reliable and versatile fabrics that are perfect for beginners. Lightweight fabrics tend to bend and twist more easily for what you are trying to sew and are more accommodating to your projects. If your project has curves, ruffles, or intricate shapes, stick with a lightweight fabric.

Quilting cotton: It doesn't get more reliable than quilting cotton. Although this fabric is meant for quilts, it can be used for accessories and clothing as well. In fact, just about every project in this book can be made from quilting cotton. It's sturdy, behaves predictably, irons beautifully, and is perfect for beginners. You can find it in a multitude of designs and it even gets softer with every wash. Solid varieties of this cotton are called broadcloth, and versions woven with a smooth, shiny finish are called sateen cotton.

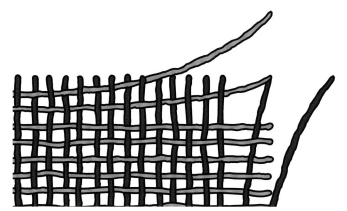

Wovens: Woven fabrics are made just like a basket, but on a much smaller scale. They're sturdy and reliable, but have the unfortunate quality of unraveling as the threads gradually pull away at the edges.

Quilting cotton: Soft, colorful, and sturdy—what's not to love about quilting cotton?

The Great Debate

Different sewers have different opinions about whether to sew garments with quilting cotton. The truth is, quilting cotton can be stiff sometimes because the fibers are densely packed to make it less likely that your quilt will fall apart after years of use. Not only that, those adorable prints often mean layers and layers of ink spread on the fabric. So stiff quilting cottons are great for stiffer items: big full skirts, dresses, and accessories. But not all fabric is created equal. Feel around your local fabric shop and you might find some subtle prints without so much ink—perfect for lighter applications like blouses and breezy dresses.

Flannel: Flannel is like the softer cousin of quilting cotton. It is the same sort of fabric used for cozy pajamas and blankets. It's still just as reliable as quilting cotton, but has a slightly fuzzy, brushed feel to it.

Shirting: This is an umbrella term used to describe fabrics that work well for shirts. They are typically made from synthetic fibers or blends, and can range in texture from smooth like quilting cotton and fluffy like flannel to puckered textures like gauze, gingham, and seersucker. They sew similarly to cotton, except they are less stiff and therefore work better for shirts.

Satin: Satin is typically made from synthetic fibers and has a quality that's often called "slinky" or "drapey." If you pinch the middle of the fabric and hold it up, you'll see that the surrounding fabric drapes completely with almost no stiffness. This drapey quality, in addition to the beautiful sheen, is what makes satin such a luxury. Unfortunately, this is also what makes satin move so unpredictably while you sew. It takes a bit of practice to get used to satin, so start out with small projects after you've honed your skills with more stable fabrics.

Flannel: A definite go-to for a softer, thicker version of quilting cotton.

Satin: While thin and tricky to sew, satin is a real luxury when you get used to its quirks under the machine.

Shirting: Less stiff than quilting cotton, shirting is perfect for garments that are a bit breezier.

About Metric

Throughout this book, you'll notice that every measurement is accompanied by a metric equivalent. Inches and yards are rounded off to the nearest half or whole centimeter unless precision is necessary. Please be aware that while this book will show 1 yard = 100 centimeters, the actual conversion is 1 yard = 90 centimeters, a difference of about 3 15/16" (10cm). Using these conversions, you will always have a little bit of extra fabric if purchasing by the metric quantity.

Medium-weight wovens

Medium-weight fabrics can't conform to as many shapes and details as lighter-weight fabrics, but they make up for it by being heftier and great for taking on tougher tasks.

Linen: Linen is a similar fabric to cotton, being very easy to work with and reliable. It's made from a natural fiber (flax), though synthetic blends are very common and can change the feel of the fabric. It's associated with the noticeable woven fibers that run through it, and it often has a drapey quality.

Linen: With a sturdy thickness but a drapey feel, linen is the best of both worlds. And the distinct threads give it a charming shabby-chic quality.

Corduroy: Corduroy is a fabric similar to twill that has raised "cords" with a velvet-like texture. It sews up nicely, although care must be taken that the cords run in the right direction in the finished product. This is called the nap, and means the direction where stroking the fabric feels smooth and natural (like an animal's coat). Various prints and colors are becoming popular with this fabric, making it great for accessories as well as clothes.

Corduroy: Like a luxurious cousin of twill, corduroy works nicely for touchable accessories, as well as clothes.

Twill & denim: Twill is a kind of woven fabric that is defined by the diagonal weave present in the fabric texture (so denim is a kind of twill). However, it can best be described as the fabric used for khaki pants or light jackets. It is often made from cotton, although stretchable synthetics and blends are common. It sews very predictably, though its thickness makes it a little less forgiving. Fabrics similar to twill are often found with the name bottomweights.

Twill: Denim and twill are perfect for sturdy, simple projects.

Brocade: Brocade is a kind of satin with layers of embroidery in the woven fabric. It's much more stable than its thinner cousins, so although sewing with satin can be tricky, brocades can be rather kind to beginners by comparison. Besides that, it's hard to turn down all those gorgeous colors and patterns.

Brocade: Give your first satin project a colorful Chinese or Indian twist with brocaded and sari fabrics.

Heavyweight wovens

The average person typically encounters heavyweight fabrics through furniture and home textiles. Very few garments are made from heavyweight fabric, and this is because heavyweight fabrics don't handle intricate curves, folds, or ruffles as well. Fabrics like these work better on a large scale, or if not that, at least with straight, simple lines with few curves and corners. So while heavyweight fabrics are typically harder to work with, here are some suggestions that should encourage you to experiment.

Canvas: Typically made from cotton or linen, canvas is a thick fabric with a very large weave. It tends to be stiff and difficult to sew through, but with the right sewing needle, the results are strong and sturdy. It is also known as cotton duck.

Home décor fabrics: This is an umbrella term that covers various thick and printed varieties of fabrics for curtains and upholstery. Smooth solid and printed varieties of twill and canvas work nicely for bags and totes. However, heavily embroidered and plush varieties can overcomplicate your project and make sewing difficult, so steer clear of those.

Faux suede: This fabric is a bit of a guilty pleasure for me, and I snatch it up whenever I find it. The texture is wonderful and the range of colors available for this fabric is amazing. This suede substitute is made from adhering a suede-like nap onto a woven fabric. It sews very well, though ironing can sometimes damage the surface. At stores it might also be called suedecloth or ultrasuede.

KNIT FABRICS

Knit fabrics are constructed differently from woven fabrics in that they are created by knitting threads to form the fabric. This is similar to the way a sweater is made (but on a much smaller scale) and is exactly what you find in your favorite t-shirts. Knit fabrics are special in that they stretch, usually horizontally along the fabric, but sometimes both horizontally and vertically. Because of this, knits are typically used for clothing and wearable accessories, because they conform to the shape of the body. Sewing knits is a bit of a challenge all its own, so tips for sewing with knits can be found later in the book (page 137).

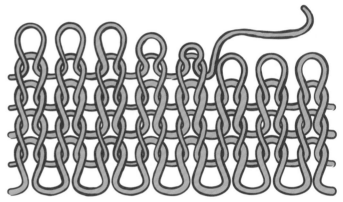

Knit fabrics: Threads are knitted together to create knit fabrics, which have the wonderful quality of stretching to fit snugly but not unraveling.

Heavyweight fabrics: Fabrics like canvas, simple home décor fabrics, and faux suede are great heavyweights for beginners.

Lightweight knits

Jersey: This is the name to look for when you consider a thin t-shirt fabric. It's manufactured with a right side (the flat, or knit side if you are a knitter) and a wrong side (the piled or purl side). It is extremely stretchy along the horizontal axis, which can make it tricky to sew, but results in a very lovely drape. It comes in cotton and synthetic blends and is sometimes called single knit.

Lycra/spandex: These fabrics are similar to jersey in their weight, yet they are made from synthetic materials like polyester, nylon, rayon, and Lycra. They sometimes stretch in four directions, making fit easier. This is what's used to make swimsuits and leotards, a challenging project for when your skills progress!

Jersey: When you think of a thin and comfy t-shirt, you're probably thinking of jersey knit.

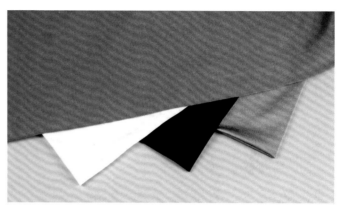

Lycra & spandex: These fabrics are much like jersey, but often stretch in four directions and are made from synthetic fibers.

Medium-weight knits

Interlock: This fabric is knitted in the same way as jersey, but it is knitted in two layers so both sides are finished to look smooth. Because the fabric is thicker, it doesn't stretch nearly as much, so there's less drape, but it's also somewhat easier to work with. This fabric comes in a great abundance of natural fibers and synthetic blends.

Fleece: Fleece is a polyester fabric with a soft nap knitted into the base of the textile. This popular fabric can be seen in a lot of store-bought jackets, hats, and mittens and sews very easily for beginners. While it stretches enough to fit well, the stretchiness doesn't affect how it sews, so I can't recommend it enough for all your warm and fluffy projects. It's also available in a plethora of solid colors and prints.

Interlock: With no wrong side, interlock is like double-sided jersey.

Fleece: Thick, plush, and comfy, fleece is the perfect way to break into sewing with knits.

This chart sums up the qualities of most fabrics you'll encounter. Use it as a quick go-to guide when deciding what you'd like best for your project!

	Fabric	Pros	Cons	Applications	Other names/ similar fabrics
Wovens — Lightweight	Quilting cotton	Sews easily, forgiving	Sometimes stiff	Bedclothes, bags, shirts, skirts, pajamas, dresses	Broadcloth, sateen, voile, lawn
	Flannel	Soft, sews easily	Tends to pill	Bedclothes, pajamas	Plaid shirting, flannel-backed satin
	Shirting	Crisp, textured	Less breathable	Shirts, dresses, belts & similar accessories	Gingham, seersucker, crepe, poplin
	Satin	Smooth, drapey	Slippery, delicate	Dresses, tops, skirts	Charmeuse, dupioni, chiffon
Wovens — Medium-weight	Linen	Drapey, textured	Unravels easily	Shirts, dresses, skirts, bags	Suiting fabric, wool, rayon
	Twill	Crisp, sews easily	Less forgiving	Slacks, skirts, light jackets, bags, accessories	Bottomweights, denim, sateen twill
	Corduroy	Soft, crisp, sews easily	Distinctive nap	Skirts, light jackets, bags, accessories	Thin chenille, embossed fabrics
	Brocade	Lustrous, crisp	Unravels easily, not forgiving	Skirts, light jackets, bags, accessories, belts, dresses	Bridal satin, taffeta, sari fabric
Wovens — Heavyweight	Canvas	Dense, strong, crisp	Not forgiving	Bags, belts, accessories	Cotton duck, burlap
	Home décor fabrics	Dense, strong, crisp	Not forgiving	Bags, belts, accessories	Upholstery fabric, printed twill, canvas
	Faux suede	Soft, crisp, sews easily	Doesn't iron well	Skirts, jackets, bags, accessories, belts	Suedecloth, ultrasuede
Knits — Lightweight	Jersey	Drapey, soft	Stretches while sewing	T-shirts, skirts, dresses, activewear	Single knit, thermal knit
	Lycra	Drapey, four-way stretch	Stretches while sewing	T-shirts, skirts, dresses, activewear, bathing suits	Tricot, spandex, nylon knit, rayon knit
Knits — Medium-weight	Interlock	Stable, breatheable	Less stretch, less drape	T-shirts, skirts, dresses, activewear, accessories	Double knit, rib knit, sweater knit
	Fleece	Stable, soft, forgiving	Less stretch, tends to pill	Jackets, hats, plush toys, accessories	Sweatshirt knit, microfleece, minky

CLOSING THE DEAL: BUYING YOUR FABRIC

When it actually comes down to buying your fabric, it's best to go in with a plan. All the colors and textures in a fabric store can be overwhelming if not tempting, and if you don't have a basic plan for what you need, you might end up with a whole lot of fabric but nothing for the quilt you intended to make.

Fabrics at typical fabric stores sell their fabrics rolled up on slats of cardboard (called *bolts*) or large rolls of fabric. Don't be afraid to feel around all the different fabrics and get acquainted with their textures. Just like trying on clothes, you want to get familiar with the fabric as much as you can before investing your money in it.

Notice how the fabric falls when you pick up a corner of it, whether it's stiff, smooth, drapey, or stretchy. How much does it wrinkle when you scrunch it? If it's destined to be a bag, can you imagine carrying it around? If it's fated to be a skirt, how does it look draped around your waist? How comfortable is the fabric? An old knitter's trick is to rub a bit against your neck; if it feels scratchy, then you probably won't enjoy wearing it. Natural fibers tend to get a little softer after their first wash, but don't purchase something that won't be fun and easy to wear.

Most fabrics come in widths of either 45" (114.5cm) or 60" (152.5cm). You get to decide the length by requesting the number of yards. Ultimately you end up with more fabric when you choose wider varieties. At fabric shops, you can typically have fabric cut in increments as small as ⅛ yd. (12.5cm). But, of course, it never hurts to get more than you need. Be sure to check out the remnant bin at your local fabric store. These bins are filled with pre-cut bits of fabric of a few yards or less at reduced prices. And don't forget the clearance section! You'll find loads of opportunities to experiment with different kinds of fabric when you're ready to move beyond old standbys.

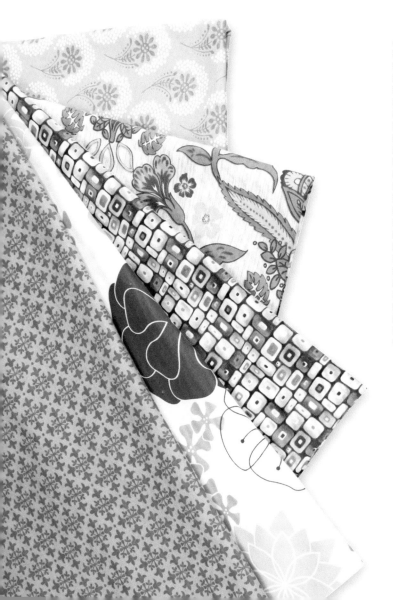

Control Your Fabric Destiny!

Of course don't let the chart on page 24 hold back your creativity! While learning to sew, being limited to fabric choices was one thing I hated! I made full mandarin dresses from upholstery brocade and slacks from plaid flannel—really strange stuff that was fun to show off, but sometimes did not hang or feel right on my skin. These suggestions are meant to make sure you get the most out of your fabric and time invested. Going on your own will get you some truly unique creations, but be warned that you might end up with an oddity or two that won't work harmoniously with your wardrobe.

Cool and Coordinated:
A Bit on Color & Design Theory

I know you don't need me to tell you how to pick your favorite colors, but if you bear with me, I can show you how to make color combinations you might not have thought of and that can help solidify your look. Without a sense of direction, you might end up with a neon orange and avocado green skirt that you can't ever imagine yourself wearing.

I'm sure you got acquainted with the color wheel in school, but it's truly underrated. By working with a plan, you can pick out some really dazzling color schemes that are completely new to you. Below are some different ways you can use it to choose a color scheme that works.

Once you've chosen your colors, experiment with tints, shades, and neutrals. Decide which color will be the focus or accent and tone down the other colors to make the accent colors pop. Neutrals don't always have to be gray, brown, and black—they are also less intense shades of a color. Dark, neutral colors tend to recede into the background, while bright, intense colors tend to advance.

Finally, as you narrow down your decision, consider how your fabric will look in the finished project. Will it be in a tiny wallet or a full-length dress? Prints and patterns work best when they are proportional to the items they make. Small items, like bags, pouches, or accessories are better suited to small prints, while large items, like curtains, blankets, or dresses, carry large prints better. Accessories are essentially accent pieces and are good for particularly bright and loud colors, as they're so small they add a bit of pop to your overall outfit.

The Color Wheel: Good old Roy G. Biv. This ring of hues will take you leaps and bounds toward really fabulous color combinations.

Complementary color scheme: A pair of colors that are opposite each other on the color wheel.

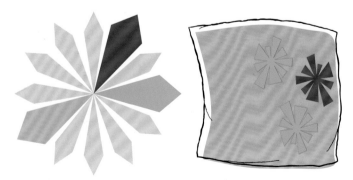

Split complementary color scheme: One hue plus the two colors adjacent to its complement.

Analogous color scheme: A set of colors adjacent to each other on the color wheel.

Conversely, neutral colors work better with larger items, as they don't shock the eye too much. A long, neutral skirt can work as a background to a more exciting electric blue belt.

In both cases, consider that the project will be viewed from many angles and distances. Most people will see your handmade top from relatively far away, so see how your fabric looks if you step back a few yards. If you're nearsighted like me, a good cheat is to slip off your glasses. If the fabric looks great both blurry and close up, you're in business!

Keep Creating!

If you're an art nerd like me, check out *colorschemedesigner.com*. It's a wonderful, interactive resource for creating color schemes based on basic color theories.

Make it you! The dusty purple sets the perfect background for rich teal and bright gold in this triangle color scheme.

Triangle color scheme: Three colors that form a triangle on the color wheel.

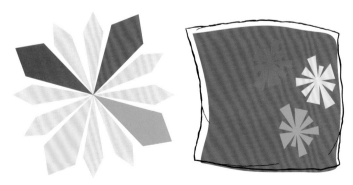

Tetrad color scheme: A pair of complementary colors that form a rectangle on the color wheel.

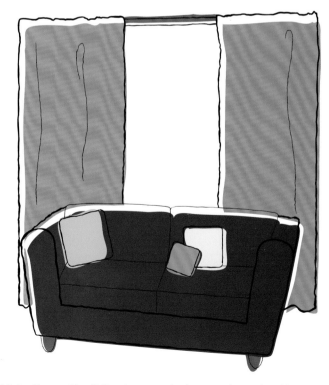

Make it practical! See how neutral magenta makes the green pillows pop in this take on a split complementary color scheme?

Choose Your Weapons:
Sewing Tools

They make dozens and dozens of persnickety and sophisticated tools for sewing, and the truth is, you really don't need most of them. A few good, reliable tools are all you need to turn out great projects. Most of them can even work double duty—a real boon, because the sewing industry is one filled with uni-taskers. These are the absolute essentials you'll need to get started with sewing, and can be considered your go-to sewing kit. We'll cover other supplies and tools later in the book, but for now here are the very basics.

BASIC SEWING KIT

Sewing machine: Check back earlier in the book (page 14) to learn how to buy and what to look for in a great sewing machine that you can rely on for years to come.

    Sewing shears: Unlike regular scissors, sewing shears are much sharper and, when taken care of properly, can cut through fabric like butter. Avoid cutting paper with them because this will dull the blade quickly. You don't have to go expensive to get the job done, but the more expensive, higher-quality shears can last a lifetime (with sharpening) and are ideal if you want to sew further down the line.

    Craft scissors: A typical pair of comfortable scissors work fine as craft scissors. Use these to cut paper patterns, thread, or any other material that would dull sewing shears.

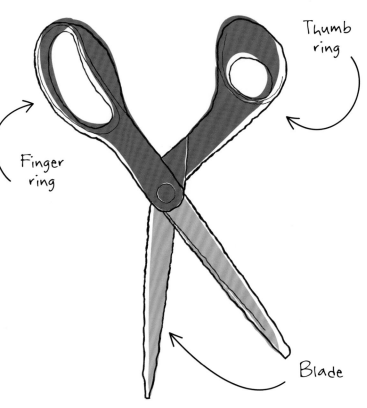

Thumb ring

Finger ring

Blade

Shears: Even an inexpensive pair will cut much better than anything in your junk drawer. Take good care of them and they'll take good care of you!

Tape measure or ruler: Sewing doesn't have to be an exact science, but it's good to have a ruler around so you know you are accurately making your project to the size you want. A tape measure is a necessity when sewing clothes or other large projects. You'll want the flexible fabric kind; they're extremely cheap, so it doesn't hurt to have more than one if the sewing bug has really bitten you. For rulers, a yardstick often does the trick, but if you're willing to spend the extra money on a transparent quilting ruler you'll find it's very helpful for cutting pattern pieces.

Seam ripper: This strange-looking tool is for picking out and cutting stitches in seams you'd like to undo. Even the best of us make mistakes, so don't be afraid to use one. See the Dealing with Mistakes section (page 57) to learn how to use one of these little buggers.

Iron: Ironing is really crucial for professional-looking results in projects made with crisp fabrics such as cotton, twill, and the like. Even a cheap iron can do the job, but more expensive irons are a good investment if you plan to sew for years. Higher-quality irons are heavier (to make pressing and creasing easier), have more precise heat settings, and also have steam and spray functions.

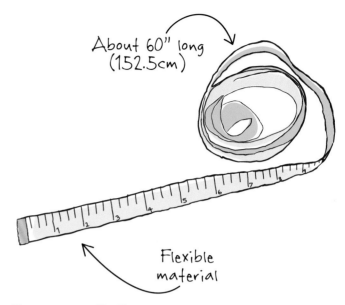

About 60" long (152.5cm)

Flexible material

Tape measure: You'll never see a sewer without one!

Seam ripper: A little tool that makes a world of difference!

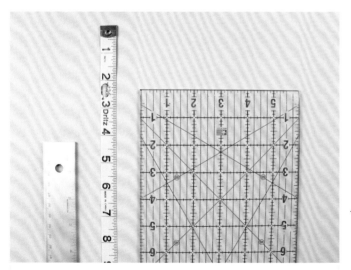

Rulers & tape measures: You'll need these to measure accurate cuts in your fabric.

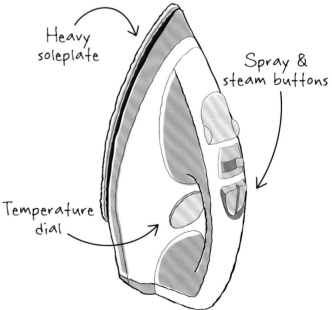

Heavy soleplate

Spray & steam buttons

Temperature dial

Iron: Often the difference between a homemade look and a professional look.

Fabric marker: If there's one little tool that will save you from sewing headaches, it has to be the fabric marker. These pens are made with disappearing (or water-soluble) ink that can be used to draw on your fabric. You can use these to mark places for buttons, zippers, pockets, or anything else that needs to be matched up on your main fabric. You might think it's unnecessary, but you'd be surprised how a little mark can go a long way. Consider getting a light-colored pencil for dark fabrics and a dark marker for light fabrics.

Sewing pins: These little guys are used for temporarily holding pieces of fabric together while you sew. They come in different lengths and degrees of sharpness, but beginners should be more comfortable with larger, longer pins with the big plastic heads. They sometimes leave slightly noticeable holes in your fabric, but you can work your way up to smaller, less obtrusive pins as you get comfortable.

Pins, needles & thread: The glue that holds all your projects together.

Washes off in water

Fabric marker: Draw all over your project and no one ever has to know!

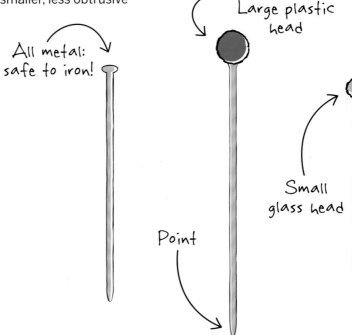

All metal: safe to iron!

Large plastic head

Small glass head

Point

Sewing pins: Large plastic-headed varieties are perfect for beginners, but go for what makes you comfortable.

You can never have too much!

Like fabric and thread, you can never have too many sewing needles! Ideally, you should replace sewing needles after every project. They get dull quickly and can pose a breaking hazard if you sew with them too long after they've dulled. At least get a new needle when you start to hear your current one is getting old. You should be able to hear a THUNK sound with each stitch your machine makes. Then you know it's a good time to move on.

Sewing machine needles: Your sewing machine needs a special kind of needle that fits specifically into your machine. They are made to suit different thicknesses of fabric in both knit and woven varieties. They are assigned a number between 8 and 19 (American) or 60 and 120 (European), with the low numbers in the range for light fabrics and the higher number for heavier fabrics. Specialty needles take care of leather or metallic embroidery. The best thing to do if you are confused is to read the package, which usually describes what the needle is for. Universal needles, around size 10–11, are perfect for beginners, but if you're venturing out into new fabric realms, try to find a needle that matches your selection the best. Read more about them in the Get to Know Your Machine section (page 34) and Your First Seam section (page 48).

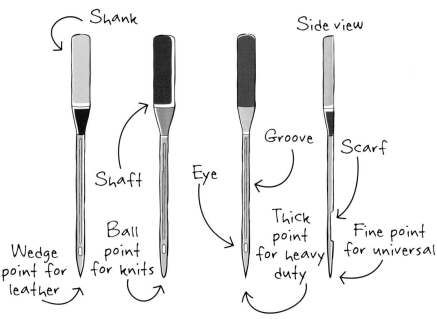

Sewing machine needles: Depending on the brand of machine needle, the shank and shaft may be colored to correspond with the type of needle.

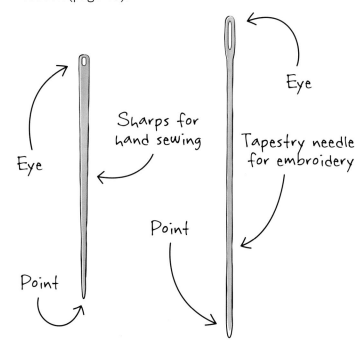

Hand sewing needles: What started all these sewing shenanigans in the first place.

Hand-sewing needles: There are specific needles for hand sewing, and these are called "sharps." They come in a range of sizes, though as the needles get larger, they are usually labeled for embroidery and tapestry sewing. Find a size that feels comfortable for you within the sharps range.

Thread: Thread is the glue that's going to hold all your projects together, so it's good to get acquainted with it. While there are quite a few different forms of thread out there, be sure to look for all-purpose thread. This is a polyester blend of thread that works wonderfully for everything. Shiny rayon threads are meant for embroidery and all cotton threads for hand quilting, which isn't what we need here for basic sewing. You will want to pick a thread that matches your fabric so contrasting colors don't peek out of your project. To see if your thread matches your fabric, hold a length of the thread across the fabric and see if it blends in. If you can't find the perfect color, go with a shade darker rather than lighter.

Construct Your Castle:
Your Sewing Space

Now that you have your sewing machine, fabric, and supplies in place, it's time to find out where you'll be doing all that awesome sewing! Not everyone can have a dedicated sewing space, but there's a good chance you can find a comfortable place to settle down somewhere in your home.

When it comes to setting up your sewing space, here are some things you should look for:

Sturdy table and chair: A desk or dining room table works well for this. Most people prefer to have their sewing machine a little high, but any height that allows you to sit up straight and comfortably while still being able to see your work is ideal. A comfortable chair is also a plus. I really prefer a computer chair because I can adjust its height and depth, and can swivel to reach other things. You can use the same surface to cut your fabric, as you can just set your sewing machine on the floor temporarily while you spread your fabric out on the table.

Good light: Your eyes will be forced to focus on tiny objects while sewing, so ample light can do wonders. A large window is perfect, but an overhead light source or side floor lamp also does the trick. If you ever find yourself squinting or getting headaches, it can really help to open some windows or bring out a desk lamp.

Spot for ironing: As you learn later on in this section, ironing is really essential for achieving professional-looking projects. If sewing is just an occasional hobby for you, ironing works just fine on a table with a towel or ironing pad protecting the surface from the hot iron. If you have the space and investment for an ironing board, however, it's very much worth it. Keep it near your sewing space, because you'll be using it a lot.

Organization: You might find yourself accumulating more fabric and tools than you planned (like with any hobby!). To keep them from overwhelming you, consider some organizational options.

Plastic totes that fit in your closet or under your bed are perfect for large pieces of fabric. Be sure to fold or roll them up nicely so they don't get badly wrinkled. You can also hang up fabric along with the rest of your clothes on a hanger.

Consider over-the-door storage pockets for small tools, thread, and the like. If you can hang the pockets near your workspace, you're really set! Of course, even shoeboxes coupled with plastic sandwich bags can get you organized in a snap.

Tiny Apartment Blues

If your domicile is more cave than castle, it helps to replace your light bulbs with high-efficiency pure white fluorescent light bulbs (25-watt or higher). They're much brighter and are closer to natural light than other bulbs. They can usually be found in hardware stores and are worth the extra cost because they last so long.

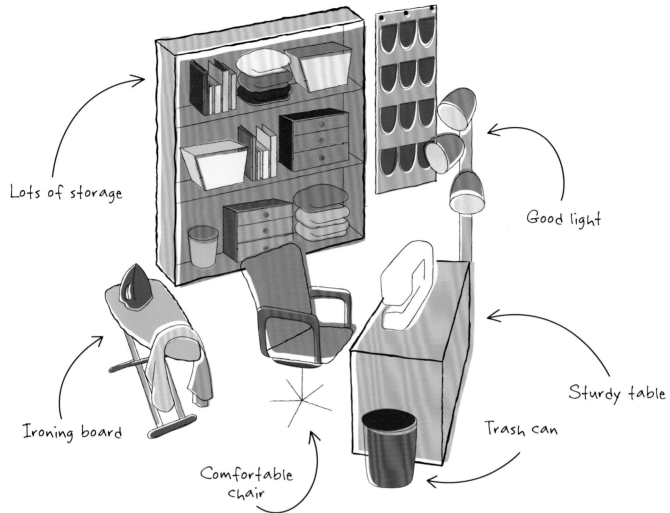

Lots of storage

Good light

Ironing board

Sturdy table

Comfortable chair

Trash can

Your sewing space: Try to find a place for all your work—the more comfortably arranged, the better.

Ouch!
Preventing Injuries

Like it or not, injuries are sometimes part of the territory when it comes to sewing. There are loads of ways to prevent minor injuries in the sewing room.

Stay alert: If you are tired, frustrated, or otherwise unfocused, try to take a break from sewing or at least from working with your machine. You want to be completely alert to what's going on around you to prevent accidents.

Keep good posture: Try to keep your posture upright and proper at all times. You can get strain on your back, elbows, wrists, and neck with improper posture.

Be cognizant of your fingers: When your sewing machine is running, be aware of where the needle is and where your fingers are. Keep them at least a few inches away from the moving needle. Be aware of what you're cutting with sharp scissors, and keep conscious of where you're poking your pins and needles. Knowing that your instruments are hazardous is one thing, but before you cut or pierce always think twice and ask yourself, "Are my fingers and hands anywhere near where this will go?"

Best Friends Forever:
Get to Know Your Machine

With any luck, you will likely have a manual that came with your machine. And while you may be tempted to skim, you really should read over your manual before trying to tinker around with your new machine. If your machine is secondhand, you might not have the luxury of a manual, but it doesn't hurt to check the manufacturer's website, where they might have a downloadable copy that pertains to your make and model.

Although every sewing machine make and model is different, here I'll do my best to get you started on your machine if finding the manual isn't an option.

The anatomy of a seam: Unlike a hand-sewn seam, which is made with one thread, a machine-sewn seam is made with two interlocking threads that form a chain. The top thread comes from your main thread spool and the bottom comes from the bobbin. With the proper tension, these two threads meet together between each stitch within the thickness of the fabric.

The anatomy of a machine: If you get to know how your machine does what it does, you'll be less likely to get frustrated with any issues you might encounter. Think of your machine as a beloved old car. You want to know everything that makes it tick so you can fix as many problems as you can by yourself instead of always taking it back to the dealership.

Power switch: When your machine is sufficiently powered and plugged in, this turns the machine on. Usually a light above your needle will switch on (check to make sure it isn't burnt out), and the machine will move when you step on the foot pedal.

Foot pedal: This is the sensor that controls the motion of your machine. Back before sewing machines were powered by electricity, the foot pedal was literally pumped with one's foot to keep the machine going. Now the machine is powered by the amount of pressure you apply to the pedal, just like the gas pedal in a car. It can be scary giving it a try at first, but with practice you can find the speed that makes you comfortable. In fact, try pressing it with bare feet, because you will be more sensitive to the pressure you apply. I personally always sew this way!

Flywheel: Also called the handwheel, the flywheel is a way of manually moving the machine without the foot pedal. When turned toward you, it moves the needle up and down. Try to avoid moving it backward, as this can cause complications in your stitches. It's good to get a feel for the flywheel because it gives you much more control, and you can easily move the needle where it needs to be without messing with the foot pedal. I've done some projects that required such careful precision that I used only the flywheel to sew them!

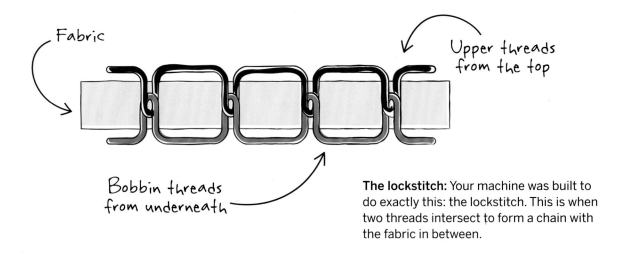

Fabric

Upper threads from the top

Bobbin threads from underneath

The lockstitch: Your machine was built to do exactly this: the lockstitch. This is when two threads intersect to form a chain with the fabric in between.

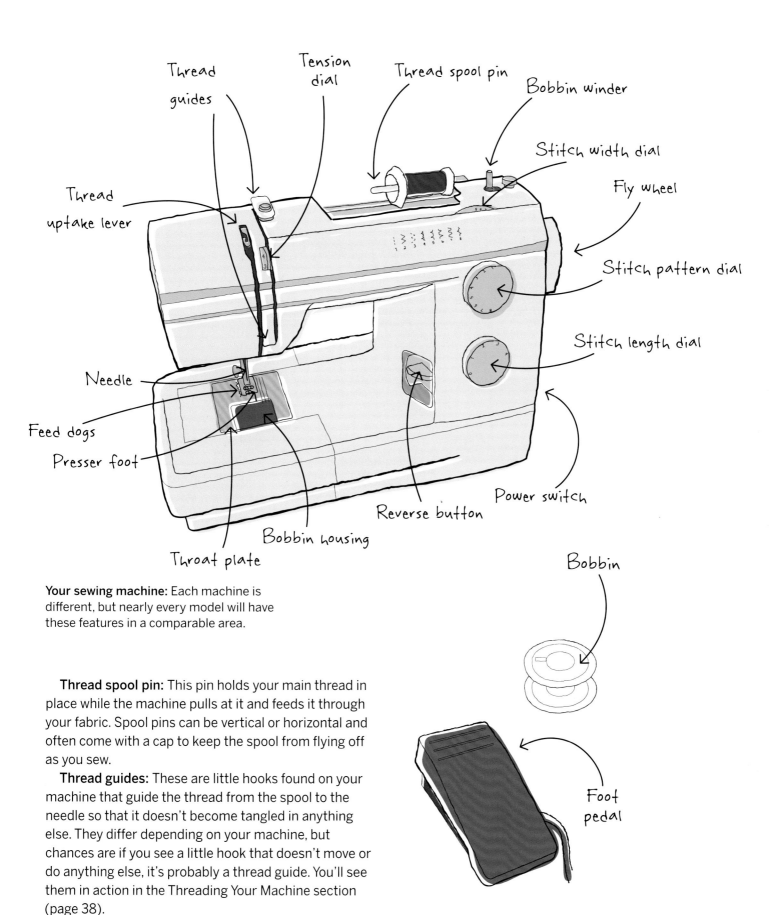

Thread guides

Tension dial

Thread spool pin

Bobbin winder

Stitch width dial

Fly wheel

Thread uptake lever

Stitch pattern dial

Stitch length dial

Needle

Feed dogs

Presser foot

Power switch

Reverse button

Bobbin housing

Throat plate

Bobbin

Your sewing machine: Each machine is different, but nearly every model will have these features in a comparable area.

Thread spool pin: This pin holds your main thread in place while the machine pulls at it and feeds it through your fabric. Spool pins can be vertical or horizontal and often come with a cap to keep the spool from flying off as you sew.

Thread guides: These are little hooks found on your machine that guide the thread from the spool to the needle so that it doesn't become tangled in anything else. They differ depending on your machine, but chances are if you see a little hook that doesn't move or do anything else, it's probably a thread guide. You'll see them in action in the Threading Your Machine section (page 38).

Foot pedal

Tension: The tension of your machine determines how tightly the thread is held as it passes through your fabric. This is done with a pair of plates that squeeze the thread with the intensity indicated on the meter. Tension can be a delicate balance that is usually handled well by the manufacturer, but in case it does need adjusted, you can read more about it after sewing Your First Seam (page 48).

Thread uptake lever: This lever pulls the thread through the tension plates so that it feeds into the needle and creates your stitch. It will move up and down while the machine sews, constantly feeding the thread.

Needle: This is where your sewing needle should be installed in your machine. It's usually screwed in place or held with some other kind of system, so be sure you have any screwdrivers you might need. Once you've loosened the screw, install the needle with the rounded side of the shank facing you and inserted as far up into the machine as it will fit. Then, tighten the screw until just snug (to avoid stripping the screw) and it should be secure enough for sewing.

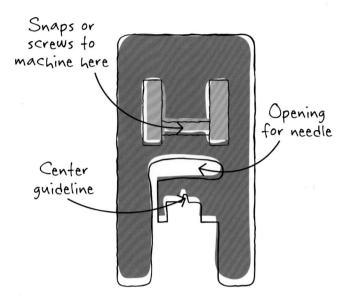

Snaps or screws to machine here

Opening for needle

Center guideline

Presser foot: This little hunk of metal not only holds down your fabric, but also has guidelines so you know exactly where your needle will be sewing.

Feed dogs: These little jagged teeth are what pull your fabric through your machine so you don't have to!

Presser foot: The presser foot is the part that holds your fabric against the feed dogs while you sew. It is controlled by a lever that is either behind the needle or to the side that moves it up and down. Always be sure to sew while the presser foot is down to get the right tension in your stitches. A basic presser foot can handle most projects, but your machine might also come with a buttonhole foot or zipper foot, which we'll tackle later. Most presser feet are held to the machine by a screw. Other presser feet snap on. Either way, make sure any screws around your presser foot are securely tightened for the safest sewing.

Feed dogs: This strange name is given to the toothed metal plates that live beneath your presser foot. When the foot pedal is pressed, these teeth grip the fabric and move it forward, similar to a conveyor belt or treadmill. That means the machine actually moves the fabric for you as you sew! If you have a machine that drops the feed dogs, you'll be able to move the fabric freehand where you want it to go—very fun for experimenting!

Throat plate: This is the metal plate that sandwiches your fabric between the presser foot and feed dogs. This plate often has engravings on it that list measurements for different seam allowances. For more, see Your First Seam (page 48).

Bobbin housing: This is the part of your machine that holds the bobbin spool. The majority of bobbin housings use a drop-in loading method. You may encounter other kinds of housings if your machine is much older or an uncommon brand.

Bobbin: This is the spool that holds your secondary thread source and forms the stitch chain with your top thread. Over time you'll fill them up with thread for each project and start amassing a collection. Unlike sewing machine needles, which tend to be interchangeable, bobbins are specific to brand. Bring a spare with you the next time you shop for more and compare them to what you see in the store. Without examples they all tend to look like they have the same shape when they are actually quite different.

Bobbin winder: Most every machine comes with an added feature of being able to wind its own bobbins. When an empty bobbin is locked into the winder, you can use the machine to wind thread from your main spool onto the bobbin. Turn to Prepping Your Machine (page 38) to see this in action.

Stitch pattern dial: This dial changes what kind of pattern the machine will make while sewing. The patterns can range from zigzag and stretch stitches to decorative stitches depending on your make and model. The dial will usually have symbols that display the different patterns to show your options. The location of the pattern, length, and width dials can vary depending on the make and model, but they're usually located near the top and sides of the machine for easy access while working.

Stitch length dial: This dial will determine how much the feed dogs move your fabric with every stitch, and thus the length of your stitch. Most basic machines determine stitch length with a number system from 0–5 or the like. A halfway setting is usually the best, as a zero setting almost doesn't move the fabric at all and the maximum setting creates very long stitches that can rip out easily.

Stitch width dial: This dial determines how far left and right from center the needle moves while making its stitch. A zigzag stitch is a basic example of this, but lots of other specialty and decorative stitches can be adjusted for width with this dial. The dial will usually read from 0–5 or the like, where 0 is no width (or minimum width for specialty stitches) and the maximum setting is the maximum width your needle can move without hitting the throat plate.

Reverse button: This button allows you to stitch backward to create what's called back tacking. Every time a seam is started, for about ¼"–½" (1–1.5cm), you should use this button to sew backward over the previous stitches, and then let go to sew forward again and on. This creates a very stable knot at the beginning of your seam that is less likely to come loose. You can see this in action in Your First Seam (page 48).

Gear Up!
Prepping Your Machine

Now that you know what makes your machine tick, there are a few prepping measures you need to take before you can sew your first seam. You'll need to get the hang of threading your machine and your bobbin. Your sewing machine guide can help you through this process, but if it's not as detailed as you'd like or missing altogether, this general guide can help you.

THREADING YOUR MACHINE

Your spool of thread should rest on the spool pin at the top of your machine, and from there it needs to travel through the tension plates, thread uptake lever, and then the needle. These are the main parts you need to worry about. Each machine will also have thread guides along the way to be sure that the thread doesn't get caught up in any other parts while it feeds through the machine.

To break down your typical threading process, you will first pull your thread off the spool pin and pull it taut against the first thread guide. You might hear a click as it snaps into place. It then goes through the tension plates, where you might hear a ping as it hits the metal. Another thread guide brings it back up to the thread uptake lever. Keep pulling it taut against the opening in the uptake and it will snap in place. Then, pull it down through more thread guides and finally through the needle. You can use your needle-threading feature if you have one, or get used to poking it through the eye. Cut the end of the thread at a slant and moisten it to get it through easily.

Threading your machine: Every machine is different, but nearly every model will have a few thread guides.

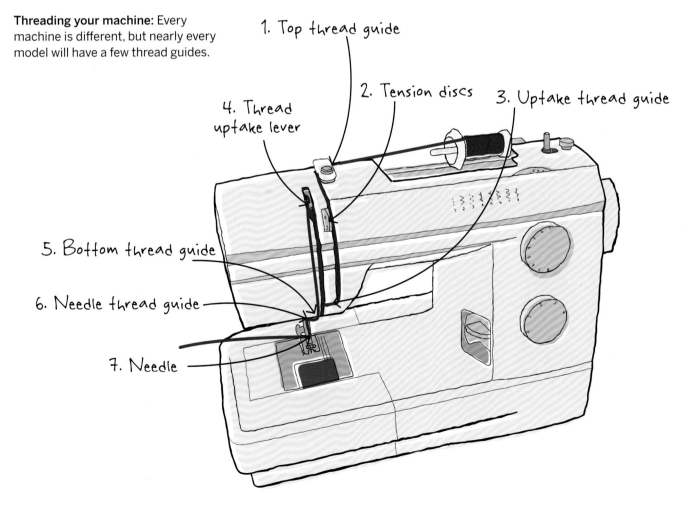

1. Top thread guide

2. Tension discs

3. Uptake thread guide

4. Thread uptake lever

5. Bottom thread guide

6. Needle thread guide

7. Needle

WINDING THE BOBBIN

To wind a bobbin of thread the same as your main thread, start by pulling the thread from your main spool and winding it around the bobbin thread guide. Take an empty bobbin and guide the end of the thread up and out of the hole found in the bobbin top. Snap the bobbin in place on the bobbin winder while holding the top thread.

Getting the winding started will differ depending on your machine's make and model, so check with your manual if you have one. Most machines require that you push the bobbin to the side to engage the winding mode in your machine. You may also have to disengage the needle. This usually involves the flywheel—either pulling it out, pushing in the center of the flywheel, or turning a center portion of the flywheel.

While holding the thread at the top of the bobbin, begin to press down on the foot pedal, slowly at first.

It should start winding your bobbin and the needle should be disengaged. Snip the thread so it doesn't get tangled and continue winding the bobbin. Most machines will stop winding on their own, but it doesn't hurt to stop before the bobbin is completely full. It won't fit into your machine if it fills beyond the spool.

Your finished bobbin should be firmly wound with thread and not loose when you poke it with your finger. If it is incorrect, it might mean the thread wasn't wound properly through the thread guide for the proper tension. With luck, you might be able to put the bobbin on your main thread spool and just wind the thread onto a new bobbin. If not, you might have to ditch the thread, though this isn't a huge waste compared to the tangled thread you'll get from a badly wound bobbin.

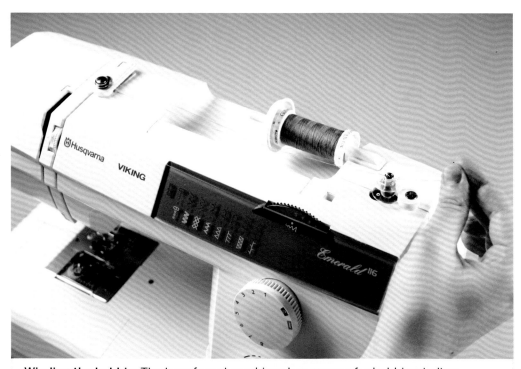

Winding the bobbin: The top of most machines has an area for bobbin winding.

LOADING THE BOBBIN

For the drop-in loading bobbin, you will need to open the bobbin housing. This usually involves sliding or unsnapping a plate from the throat plate of the machine to reveal the housing. Take the thread from your newly would bobbin and hold it so the thread unwinds clockwise. Drop it into the casing and pull the thread through the notch found in the bobbin housing. Pull the thread toward the back of the machine and you might hear a faint click. This is the thread popping into place with the bobbin tension. You should feel a bit of resistance when pulling at the thread. If not, take out the bobbin and try again.

Once the bobbin is threaded, you'll need to bring the thread up through the throat plate of the machine. Hold onto the main thread from the needle and pull it about 6" (15cm) away from the machine. Turn the flywheel so the needle dips down into the throat plate. You should see the thread come around and grab the bobbin thread as you watch the bobbin housing. You're watching a stitch being made! When the needle comes back up it should have grabbed the bobbin thread. Pull at the main thread until the bobbin thread comes out of the throat plate. Grab the bobbin thread with your fingers or a pencil and pull both threads toward the back of the machine. Pop the bobbin cover back in place and both threads will be ready and waiting for you!

Loading the bobbin: Your machine may have printed guide arrows showing how to load your bobbin.

Bringing up the bobbin thread: Hand-guiding your machine through one stitch is what brings up your bobbin thread.

A Sewer's Arsenal:
Your Machine Stitches

As I mentioned before, you can do every project in this book with a machine that only knows a zigzag and straight stitch. And it's true! Here's all that you can accomplish by just fiddling with your stitch length and width dials.

Basic stitch:

Width: 0
Length: Short to medium

This stitch is ideal for all of your general seaming needs. Go shorter for lighter, more delicate fabrics, and a bit longer for thicker, sturdier fabrics.

Basting and gathering stitch:

Width: 0
Length: Long

A straight stitch at maximum length is used for basting. This is a seam that's meant to hold fabric temporarily in place where it can't be seen or will be removed later. This is also used for gathering fabric to make items like ruffles. Learn more about that in the Gathering Fabric section (page 85).

Buttonhole stitch:

Width: Narrow
Length: Short

A narrow and short zigzag stitch is what's used when making a buttonhole. Most machines come equipped with a feature to do this automatically, but if yours doesn't, it can be made freehand with this stitch.

Stretch stitch:

Width: Narrow
Length: Medium to long

A narrow zigzag with a longer length is used as a basic stretch stitch. When sewing knit fabrics, your finished seams will stretch along with the fabric when sewn with these stitches.

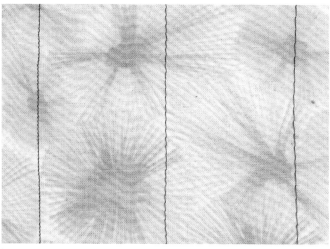

Straight stitches: Vary your stitch length to get short stitches suitable for fine fabrics, medium-length stitches for light- to medium-weight fabrics, and long stitches for basting and gathering.

Zigzag stitches: Vary your stitch length and width to get stitches for buttonholes, knit fabrics, appliqué, finishing, and couching.

Appliqué zigzag stitch:

Width: Medium to wide

Length: Short

   A medium to wide zigzag done in a short length makes a great stitch for sewing appliqué fabric. Turn to the appliqué feature (page 64) to see it in action.

Finishing stitch:

Width: Medium

Length: Medium to long

   A basic zigzag stitch is perfect for finishing the edges of your fabric so they don't unravel. This can be done within the seam allowance or over the edge of the fabric. Learn more about this in Your First Seam (page 48).

Couching stitch:

Width: Wide

Length: Medium to long

   Couching is a kind of decorative technique that sews down cords, yarn, or other embellishments to your fabric. This same technique can sew down a thin piece of ribbon or string that can be used to easily gather your fabric. Turn to the Gathering Fabric section (page 85) to see this in action.

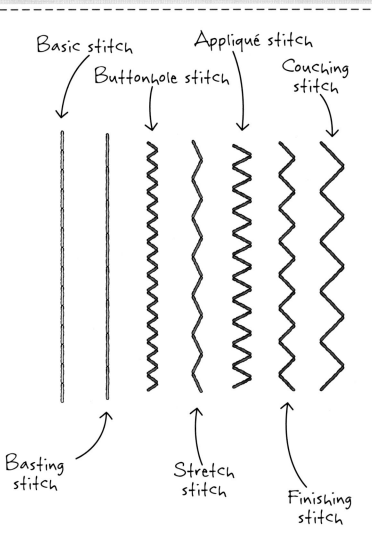

Machine stitches: Even if your machine has hundreds of stitches, just a straight and zigzag feature can make a world of projects.

	Width			
	Straight	**Narrow Zigzag**	**Medium Zigzag**	**Wide Zigzag**
Short	Stitching for delicate fabrics	Buttonhole stitch	Appliqué zigzag	Appliqué zigzag
Medium	Basic stitch	Stretch stitch	Finishing stitch	Couching stitch
Long	Basting/ gathering stitch	Stretch stitch	Finishing stitch	Couching stitch

Length

A Guided Tour:
How to Follow the Projects

Now that you know the basics of your sewing machine and the tools you'll be working with, you should be ready to dive in to your first project. The projects in this book generally work from the simplest to the most time-intensive and complex, allowing you to improve your skills as you go. There will be lots of other useful sewing techniques to learn along the way, and each technique is followed by test projects that let you test out your new skills with little investment!

With each project, you'll find a tools and materials list, listing all the fabric and other supplies you'll need, as well as in what quantities. As mentioned before, fabrics come in varying widths and the materials list will state how many yards you'll need depending on the width. If the list doesn't specify, then either width is fine. The tools you need are also listed, including your basic sewing kit and any additional tools.

Although every project is suitable for complete beginners, you'll find that they are rated from one to eight stars based on the estimated time needed, the additional techniques used, and the overall complexity of the project.

⭐ If you've never picked up a needle, start with these! They usually require one to three very easy techniques and take mere minutes to make.

⭐⭐ Your beginner's jitters have worn off and you're not so anxious to cut into your fabric anymore. These projects require one to three simple techniques or take about an hour to make.

⭐⭐⭐ You're starting to understand the basic principles and are eager to see how they work together. These projects require two to four simple techniques or take a little more than an hour or so to make.

⭐⭐⭐⭐ You've had a few ah-ha! moments and new techniques sound exciting rather than scary to you. These projects may have one or two intermediate techniques or take between one and two hours to make.

⭐⭐⭐⭐⭐ Using your machine has started to become natural, and you barely have to look at your manual or cheat sheet anymore. These projects may have two or three intermediate techniques or take two hours or so to make.

⭐⭐⭐⭐⭐⭐ Using techniques now feels completely natural and you barely have to check up on how to do them anymore. These projects may have three or four intermediate techniques or take between two and three hours to make.

⭐⭐⭐⭐⭐⭐⭐ The mechanics of sewing and assembling fabric pieces now start to make sense, and you can see where your project is going as you assemble it. These projects may have one or two advanced techniques or take about an afternoon of work to make.

⭐⭐⭐⭐⭐⭐⭐⭐ You feel like you're really in the zone and you're ready to take on anything! These projects have three or four advanced techniques or take a few afternoons of work to make.

USING THE PATTERNS

Each project comes with pattern pieces either printed in the back of the chapter or listed as squares that you should cut. The printed patterns can be enlarged at a copy center or on your personal computer so they can be cut out with craft scissors.

The printed patterns list everything you need to know so you can work with them in the easiest way possible, including the pattern piece name, the seam allowance, the seam line, the number you should cut, and what fabric and color you should cut it from, if it's applicable. Each pattern also has a grain line, which indicates in what direction the pattern should be placed when it's cut from the fabric.

For square patterns, the project will list dimensions you can use to cut the pieces straight from your fabric without requiring a pattern piece. However, because it's always smarter to measure twice and cut once, I sometimes like to measure these pattern pieces from newspaper and use those on the fabric rather than cutting straight from the material.

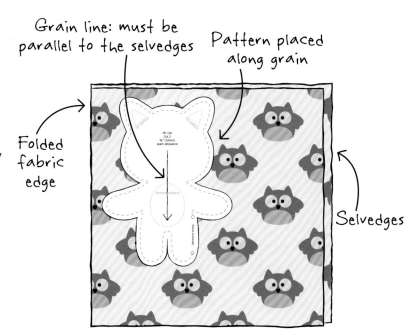

Grain line: must be parallel to the selvedges

Pattern placed along grain

Folded fabric edge

Selvedges

Placing your pattern: Always try to cut your patterns on the grain of the fabric, especially when working with a directional print.

Stars to Caffeine!

Ranking the projects with stars is very straightforward and easy to follow—perfect if you're just starting out. I must confess that I'm a bit of a foodie, though, so I often think of the level of difficulty of each project in terms of food. For example: sourness! In this case, the easiest projects might be called tangerines, and the hardest projects grapefruits. Or spiciness, where the easiest projects are green peppers and the hardest are ghost peppers! One of my favorite ways to think about project difficulty is by level of caffeine. Easier projects are perfect for working during a lazy afternoon and sipping your favorite cup of green tea, while for the harder ones, you might need to break out the espresso! If I were to translate these projects to levels of caffeine, this is what they would look like:

| White Tea | Green Tea | Black Tea | Cappuccino | Latte | Cuppa' Joe | French Roast | Espresso |

If you were to choose a way to represent a project's difficulty level, how would you do it?

PREPARING YOUR FABRIC

When you have your fabrics ready for your project, you should first be sure to prewash them if they're brand new. Fabric bolts at the store list the washing instructions, though basic beginner fabrics rarely require special washing processes. Prewashing eliminates the light starch that tends to be applied to retail fabrics, and it also gets any shrinkage out of the way.

If your fabric is wrinkle-prone, be sure to iron it smooth before cutting from it. The most typical way to cut pattern pieces is to fold the fabric in half so the selvedge edges meet. The selvedge edges are the machine-finished edges of your fabric; you'll notice that they're a lot stiffer than the rest of the fabric. Check to see if your fabric has a direction to it. If the prints or designs all point in one direction, you'll want your pattern pieces aligned so the pattern matches. It's a persnickety thing, so it's only really important with big graphics. You'd hate to have your new tote bag covered with upside-down owls! To assist with this, the grain lines on each pattern piece indicate the direction the design should point in. For the best results, make sure the grain line is parallel to the selvedge edge of your fabric.

Next, you'll want to pin your pattern pieces to your fabric exactly the same way as pinning fabric together. Weave the pins in then out of the layers of fabric and paper. Pin down all your pattern pieces at once, trying to leave as little space between them as possible to get the most out of your fabric. Because you're cutting your fabric on a folded sheet, notice that you'll get two pieces at once. This is not only a time saver, but it's typical practice in sewing, as most projects are designed to be symmetrical. Your pattern will indicate how many pieces you need to cut. It's usually two, but if not, unfold your fabric before cutting.

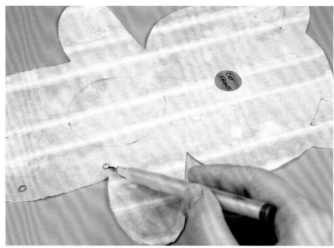

Label & mark your pieces: Transfer all the markings and notes from the pattern to your fabric and it will be a huge help as you embark on your project.

CUTTING YOUR PATTERN PIECES

Once you have all your pattern pieces pinned, it's time to cut them out. Cut as closely as possible to the outside edge of your patterns. If your scissors are sharp, you shouldn't have any issue getting clean and smooth cuts.

When all your pieces are cut from the fabric, begin to remove your patterns. Using your fabric marker, transfer any markings from the patterns to the fabric. Check the project page for any additional markings that need to be made. Another helpful trick is to label your pattern pieces. If you have adhesive labels on hand, those are perfect, but masking tape works well in a pinch. Label the right side of the fabric, and write the name of the pattern piece so you'll know when to use it. Now you'll always know what side is the right side and make sure to match it up!

All of this prep work may seem tedious, but you can take it from me that it's well worth the extra time and saves headaches and confusion in the long run. Often this start-up work takes up about half the time I spend on a project (don't worry, this time is reflected in the project time estimates!), so once you finish you can feel like you're nearly halfway there!

Waste not, want not!

Make the most of your supplies and don't throw those scraps away! Not only can small scraps be used to make some of the tinier projects in this book, but even scraps that seem useless can have a purpose! Test out your stitching on them to experiment with working on your new fabric, see if your tension is right, or just try out your decorative stitches!

1

Simple First-Time Techniques

Get your sewing career off to a fantastic start with these effortless techniques and accompanying projects. Each one is straightforward and simple to understand. Treat yourself to a delicate little sachet with appliqué or a matching set of plush cats. Or make a huge batch of sachets to give as gifts and get in loads of practice hours. With the techniques here, you'll be ready to tackle more in no time!

Skills to Master

- ☐ Your First Seam
- ☐ Dealing with Mistakes
- ☐ Hand Sewing
- ☐ Appliqué
- ☐ Sewing Curves

54 Pillow Sham

61 Bellflower Pincushion

67 Sweetly Scented Sachet

72 Marvelous Mr. & Mrs. Cat

Dive In: Your First Seam

Now that you have your fabric and supplies, and your machine all threaded, it's time to try your hand at your very first seam. Seams are a series of stitches of thread that join two (or more) pieces of fabric together. You see seams everywhere in textile products; they're what change a piece of two-dimensional fabric into the three-dimensional shapes that hold your stuff, decorate your house, or cover your body.

1 **Find the right side.** Get some scrap pieces of fabric that are about 6" (15cm) square. Decide which side will be the right side of the fabric (the outside of your finished project) and which will be the wrong side (the inside of your project). It's up to you to decide, but usually you want your image or print to be facing outward. If they both look the same, pick a side and stick to it.

2 **Align the edges.** When making any seam, the default is to put the right sides together. Unless the pattern says otherwise, this is how a seam should always be assembled. Align the edges of the two fabric pieces, right sides together.

3 **Pin the fabric.** Use your sewing pins to pin the fabric pieces together. Weave each pin in and out of the fabric one time, and that's enough to make a temporary hold. Standard practice is to place the pins perpendicular to the edge of the fabric.

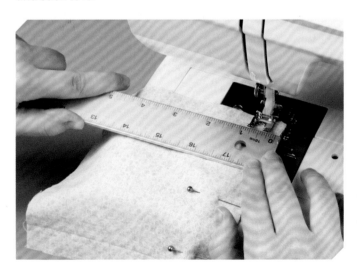

4 **Assess your seam allowance.** Your seam allowance is the amount of space between your seam stitches and the edge of the fabric; this is something to remember for every seam you make. For this test, try for a standard ⅝" (1.5cm) seam allowance. Place your fabric under the machine so the edge lines up with the seam allowance mark engraved on your throat plate.

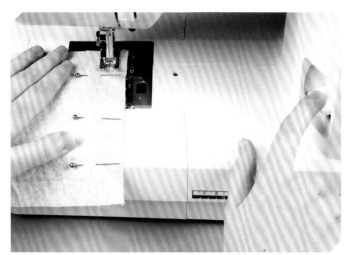

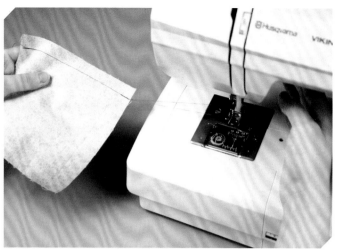

5 **Back tack your seam.** Lower your presser foot, check to see that your machine is ready to go, and begin sewing! Lightly rest your fingertips on the fabric, several inches away from the needle. Gently press on the foot pedal. Just like the gas pedal in a car, you want to start off gently and slowly and work up your speed. Use your hands to keep the fabric straight and let the feed dogs do the pulling. Sew for about ¼"–½" (0.5cm–1.5cm) and then press the reverse button. Sew backward to where you began. This is called back tacking and locks your starting stitches so they don't unravel.

6 **Complete your seam.** Continue sewing your seam, keeping the edge of the fabric lined up with the seam allowance mark on your throat plate. Be sure to remove each pin as you come to it—sewing over your pins can break your needle. When you reach the end of your fabric, repeat the back tacking procedure from Step 5. When you stop, use the flywheel to move your needle up and out of the way, lift your presser foot, pull your fabric out at least 10" (25.5cm) from your machine, and clip the thread tails.

Seam Allowances

Your seam allowance is the amount of space you leave between your seam and the edge of the fabric. It's important that you keep a consistent seam allowance while you sew to ensure that your finished product is the right size. Make your seam allowance too small, and your project will be too big, while too big a seam allowance will make your project too small. The most common seam allowance used in patterns is ⅝" (1.5cm), which you'll find in patterns for clothing and large projects. You might feel that ⅝" (1.5cm) is too big for a seam allowance, but keeping it that way gives you plenty of room to finish your seams, redo your stitching, or deal with mistakes.

Anatomy of a seam: Your typical seam should look something like this.

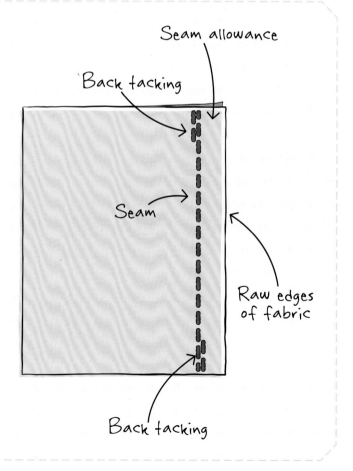

Seam allowance

Back tacking

Seam

Raw edges of fabric

Back tacking

TROUBLESHOOTING

Congratulations! You've just created your first seam! Now those two pieces of fabric have joined into one, with only a barely noticeable line showing on the right side. How does it feel to be well on your way to creating loads of awesome projects?

If you're not quite so excited, it could be because you've run into some issues. Here are some common problems:

Skipped stitches or thread is breaking: The most common solution for this is the right sewing needle. Check your needle to see if it matches the fabric you're using, and try to pick out a needle that is better suited for your fabric. If this doesn't solve the problem, you might have an issue with your machine's timing and it will need a tune-up.

Mess of tangled thread: If your stitches created less of a pretty dotted line and more of a mess of thread barf, the issue is usually in how your machine was threaded. Make sure your top thread is going through all the major machine parts (tension plates, thread uptake, and thread guides). It's sometimes hard to tell just by looking, so you might have to rethread your machine (practice makes perfect!). Also check to make sure the bobbin was threaded properly.

Fabric is puckering: Puckers are small creases and wrinkles formed in your fabric around your stitching. If you see this, it's a good time to check your tension. The top and bottom threads should be even along the fabric and you shouldn't see one thread peeking over the other side and vice versa. If the top thread shows on the bottom, try increasing the tension, and if the bottom thread shows on the top, try decreasing the tension. A tension setting of 3–5 is the norm, but if you have to go the extreme (0 or 9) to get your tension right, your machine might need a tune up.

COMPLETING SEAMS

What really separates the amateurs from the professionals is how you complete your seams. This is what keeps your project looking crisp and smooth, and holds it together for years to come.

Ironing Your Seam

Ironing is what makes your seams look neat and pretty, and less like your project was just thrown together. The directions from your project will tell you whether ironing is necessary. Whenever it's called for, try to iron your seams like this. Some projects will have unusual shapes, so you won't be able to do every step here, but try to do as much as you can for the best results.

1 **Iron the inside.** Using the heat setting suitable for your fabric, iron the completed seam on the inside or wrong side of the fabric. This should smooth out any minor puckers or warping.

2 **Iron the seam open.** From the inside or wrong side, open out the seam allowances with your fingers and iron them down.

3 **Iron the outside.** Turn the fabric over and iron the outside or right side, so the finished side of the fabric looks crisp.

Perfect corners!

Sewing corners: If you've wondered how to sew corners with your machine, it's super simple! When you reach the point at which you want to pivot, stop sewing and use the flywheel to make sure your needle is inserted into the fabric. Lift your presser foot while keeping the needle in place. Then, turn your fabric. Lower your presser foot again and keep sewing. Voila! A perfect sharp turn!

Clipping corners: When this corner is turned right side out, be sure to trim the corner seam allowance close to your stitching so the extra fabric doesn't bunch up and keep your corner from looking clean and flat. You'll hear more about this and reducing bulk in the Sewing Curves section (page 70). Poke the inside of the corner with a chopstick or similar tool for a perfect corner.

FINISHING YOUR SEAM

An unfortunate characteristic of all woven fabrics is that they unravel. When raw edges of woven fabrics are left exposed, the threads and fibers that weave and make up the fabric eventually fray and come apart over time (especially during washing). Finishing keeps the edges of your fabric from unraveling so your project lasts a good long time. A seam only has to be finished if it's exposed after the project is complete, so every project in this book will warn you when seams need to be finished. They can be finished in many ways:

Zigzag edge

Pinking: This is what it's called when pinking shears are used on fabric. Cut a scant ¼" (0.5cm) from the edges of your seam allowances. The resulting zigzag edge will fray less because the edges are cut on the bias.

Pinking shears: The zigzag pattern that pinking shears create prevents woven fabrics from fraying.

Zigzag stitch: Sew a medium width and medium length zigzag stitch within your seam allowance. The fabric will stop fraying when it reaches the zigzag stitches. If you prefer to finish each piece of fabric separately, it's best to sew the zigzag before completing your main seam.

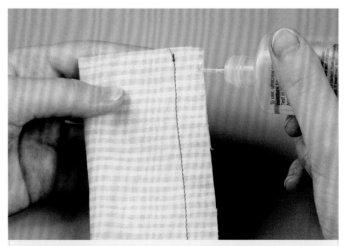

Fray block liquid: This liquid is a sealant that keeps the edges of your fabric from unraveling when it is applied to the seam allowances or other edges of the fabric. It's best used on shorter edges because it takes so much liquid to cover a long distance.

Hemming: This technique dodges the fraying edge problem entirely by encasing the raw edge of your fabric. This is not done within the seam allowances but rather along the outside edges of completed projects. The pattern will instruct you to fold the fabric over either once or twice by a specified amount. When this fold is sewn down, the raw edge of the fabric is hidden and therefore will not fray.

When to Finish

A good rule of thumb on finishing is if the raw edge is hidden within the project, and you can't see it from any angle, it won't fray! An obviously visible raw edge is susceptible to the wear and tear that causes unraveling, but a hidden one is not.

Your Little Cheat Sheet: How to Do it All Again

If you follow these steps for sewing, ironing, and finishing, you will have very successful projects that look great and last a long time. As you get started, use this cheat sheet so you start every seam off strong! Feel free to copy this and tape it to your machine, desk, or anywhere that might help you get the hang of using your machine.

☐ Do you have the right color thread?

☐ Are your top thread and bobbin threaded?

☐ Have you installed the right needle?

☐ Have you selected the right stitch type, length, and width?

☐ Are the proper sides of your fabric facing?

☐ Are your edges pinned together?

☐ Do you know where you'll start and stop sewing?

☐ Do you know your seam allowance?

☐ Is your presser foot down over your fabric?

☐ Remember to back tack the beginning and end.

☐ Remove the pins as you go.

☐ Iron your seam, if applicable.

☐ Finish your seam allowances, if applicable.

YOUR FIRST PROJECT:
Pillow Sham

ESTIMATED TIME:
20–40 minutes

TECHNIQUES:
Finishing Seams (page 52),
Hemming (page 53),
Ribbon/Trim

MAKES:
One standard 28" x 20"
(71 x 51cm) sham

You've learned just about everything a beginning sewer can handle, so it's time to start diving into projects! A pretty pillow sham is about as easy as it gets, and you can start right away at decorating your room or apartment. While it might seem boring, you can easily dress the sham up with pretty ribbon and trim. It's actually better if you don't go too crazy, because too much embellishment would irritate you as you try to sleep on the pillow. For the optional trim follow Steps 1 and 2. For a plain pillow sham, skip ahead to Step 3.

Materials

☐ 1 yd. (100cm) quilting cotton or lightweight woven fabric

☐ 1⅓ yd. (133cm) ribbon or trim (optional)

☐ Fusible web tape (optional)

Tools

☐ Basic sewing kit (see page 28)

☐ Chopstick or similar turning tool

Your collection of fabric pieces for this project should look something like this:

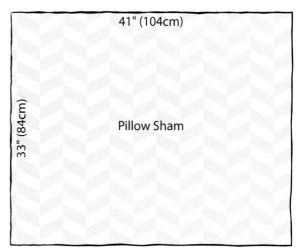

41" (104cm)

33" (84cm)

Pillow Sham

THE PREP WORK:
Cut your fabric pieces using the chart below.

Pillow Sham Pieces

Piece Name	Material to Cut	Size to Cut	Number to Cut	Seam Allowance
Sham	Quilting cotton/lightweight woven	33" x 41" (84 x 104cm)	1	⅝" (1.5cm)

Ribbon & Trim

Colorful and exciting ribbon and trim are easy ways to liven up your project with little effort. Trims are sold both by the yard and by the spool and can be sewn directly onto your project or attached with the help of fusible web. This project uses thin trim, no more than 1" (2.5cm) wide. Beginners should stick with stable trims, such as grosgrain ribbon, rickrack, or embroidered trims. Stay away from anything too fussy, lacey, sequined, or stretchy. You should be able to imagine sewing an unobstructed line all the way down the trim with your machine. If there are bits and bobs in the way, you'll have issues when you try to sew it at home.

Ribbon & trim: Sew on various trims and ribbon to get vibrant results in no time!

1 **To add trim: Fuse the trim.** On the right side, mark a line 6½" (16.5cm) in from one long edge of your sham. Center your fusible web and then your trim over this line and iron them in place according to the manufacturer's directions.

2 **To add trim: Sew the trim.** Using a straight stitch, sew the trim in place either down the center if it's very narrow or down each side if it's wider (more than ¼" [0.5cm]).

3 **Sew the side and bottom.** Fold the sham in half, right sides together, matching up the short edges. Your square of fabric should be 33" x 20½" (84 x 52cm). Sew along the short side without the trim, going toward the long side. Pivot at the corner and sew the long side, going toward the trim. Finish and iron your seam.

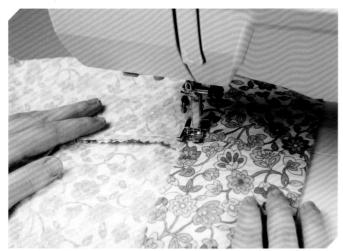

Fusible Web Tape

Fusible web tape is a great cheat for professional-looking results when adding trim! It comes in rolls of different widths and adheres two layers of fabric together with the heat of your iron. If you get a width that matches your trim, you can iron your trim in place so it holds perfectly still while you sew!

4 **Hem the opening.** Your sham should have an opening at one end. Create the double-fold hem by folding down the edge by 1" (2.5cm) and ironing it in place. Then, fold the edge down again by 3½" (9cm) and iron. Sew these folds in place. Turn the sham right side out, and poke the corners with a chopstick if necessary to define them. Congratulations! You've just made your first project! It will be as useful as it is beautiful!

Oops! Dealing with Mistakes

With any luck your first project went smoothly and painlessly, but that can't always be the case. Maybe you ran into some issues, and here's how to handle them.

Ripping out stitches: Maybe your seams weren't quite so straight or your trim turned out wonky. It's never too late to go back and rip out seams with your

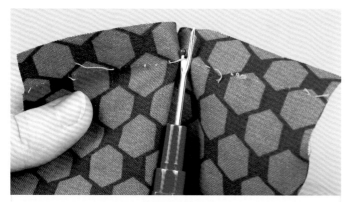

Using a seam ripper: The blade in the crook of the seam ripper makes short work of bad stitches.

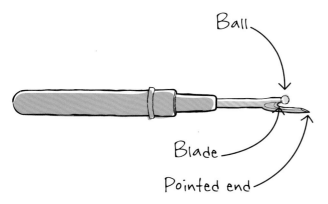

Seam ripper: This little tool with a sharp point is great for all kinds of precise cutting tasks.

handy seam ripper. The pointed blade end should be used to pick out any backstitches you've sewn. This is typically done from the top of the seam. With the rest of the stitches, open up the seam so the connecting threads show. Insert the ball end of the seam ripper between the stitches, and the blade inside the crook of the seam ripper will cut the threads. Continue pulling apart your fabric and cutting the threads until you've removed the offending seam.

Uneven edges: Perhaps you encountered edges that just wouldn't line up while you sewed. This could be caused by mistakes in measuring and often if the fabric was pulled or stretched while you were sewing. Go back and recheck your measurements to be sure you cut the shape you needed. Also, be sure to let the feed dogs do the pulling while you sew. If your project still looks all right despite the errors, you can often get away with trimming whatever fabric runs over.

Trimming uneven edges: If things don't quite line up after your seam is done, trimming a little fabric off the end is okay, as long as the project still looks fine.

CAN YOU REALLY TELL?

If your mistake is not so obvious, you might want to consider whether it's really that bad at all. Small puckers here and there, slightly uneven lines, and imperfect seams aren't nearly as noticeable as you might think. Take a look at it from far away; the average person might not even recognize an issue. Take a break from your sewing or sleep on it and see how you feel in the morning. If you learn to forgive yourself early, it makes keeping your motivation up that much easier as you encounter more projects and their assorted problems. Look at it this way: Every project you make is just practice for the next one, and everything you sew is just a stepping-stone in your journey as a sewer.

Keep Your Cool

Realizing you've made a mistake is bad enough without having to take several more minutes going back and fixing your error. It can be frustrating and even heartbreaking enough that you'll want to throw your work away. Do your best to keep from getting discouraged by taking a breather. Step away from the project for a while and play a quick computer game, get a snack, or tidy up. Then, when you're ready to undo your mistake, try ripping out those seams while watching a movie or TV show—you'll have something to occupy your mind besides your frustration.

Keeping It Old School: Hand Sewing

Every sewer (or artist of any kind) typically has one technique that they hate to the very core of their being. They constantly put it off rather than get within a foot of the process. For most sewers it's zippers or knit fabrics, but for me, it was hand sewing. I used to do everything possible to avoid hand sewing. I would change the patterns I used just so I could replace the hand sewing with machine sewing. I was convinced that hand sewing took far too long and wasn't worth the effort. But the truth was that I probably wasted more time messing with my machine to get the stitches right when just doing the hand sewing would have been much faster in the end.

I finally came around about five years into my sewing career when I was asked to make a dress for a friend. The hem had a delicate trim that needed foot after foot of hand sewing and I dreaded coming to it. When I finally had to add the trim I thought ahead and first decided to bone up on my skills. I found out there were better stitches to accomplish what I wanted, so a lot of my headaches were from ignorance! Second, I decided to take several breaks while I sewed—even if I thought I didn't need them—so there wasn't a chance I would get frustrated. Lastly, I hunkered down with a favorite movie while I worked; I already knew it by heart, so there was no chance of it distracting me.

I found all those things combined did the trick— sewing that trim was a relaxing, almost meditative experience, and now I have no qualms about whipping out the old sharps.

There are some kinds of sewing that just can't be done by machine, and certain hand-sewing stitches can do wonders. They can sew in places machines can't reach, they can sew a seam that's nearly invisible, and they can give you more control. Here are some reliable and helpful stitches that you can use throughout this book.

Preparing your needle: Use a hand-sewing needle, or sharp, in a size that you feel comfortable with. Pull a length of thread that's about two times the length of your arm. Thread one end of the thread through the needle eye. Hold both ends of the thread length and pull the needle through the thread for the full length. You should now have a length of thread, folded in half, with your needle down the middle.

Make a knot at the tail ends of your thread, or make a knot in your fabric before you start stitching. Do this by weaving the needle through a small bit of fabric, around ⅛" (0.5cm), and then pull the thread until the tail ends stick out by about 1" (2.5cm). Repeat the same stitch in the same spot, but before you tighten the stitch, loop the needle through the loop in your thread similar to a half-hitch knot.

Backstitch: This is the basic hand-sewing stitch used in place of a sewing machine stitch. After creating your knot in the thread or fabric, insert your needle into the beginning of the seam. Bring it up about ½" (1.5cm) away. Insert the needle again, going backward about ¼" (0.5cm), and then up ¼" (0.5cm) beyond the previous stitch. This is a constant "two steps forward, one step back" rhythm that creates a very neat, yet strong, seam.

Knot your thread: Instead of creating a knot at the end of your thread, it's much more secure to create one tied into the fabric itself.

Backstitch: If you need to hand sew a seam that replaces a sewing machine stitch, the backstitch is the way to go.

Basting stitch: This is a simple hand-sewing stitch that replaces the basting stitches done by your machine. You'll have much more control and can hold your fabric together without the aid of sharp pins! If you plan to remove these stitches later, avoid making a knot in your thread or fabric. Instead leave a very long thread tail to keep your seam from unraveling. Insert your needle into the beginning of the seam, and weave it back and forth through the layers going about 1" (2.5cm) per stitch.

Ladder stitch: This stitch is also known as a slip stitch, because you are slipping the needle into the folds of fabric to bring two folded edges together. This results in a nearly invisible seam that can be done from the outside of your project.

Create a knot from the inside of your project so it doesn't show, and then begin by weaving the needle in and out of one fold in your fabric, making a stitch about ¼" (0.5cm) long. Move to the next side, progressing forward, and repeat the same stitch. Tighten the stitches lightly as you go along, and you'll see the ladder shape formed by the threads will disappear into the fabric.

Create a knot at the end in the fabric, and then insert the needle beside the knot and through the project, pulling it away from your seam. Clip the thread while you pull and the thread tail will disappear into the finished project.

Basting stitch: This stitch works well for temporary seams or for making ruffles as described in the Gathering Fabric section (page 85).

Ladder stitch: Also known as a slip stitch, this creates a nearly invisible seam from the outside of your project.

Bellflower Pincushion

ESTIMATED TIME:
20–40 minutes

TECHNIQUES:
Ladder Stitch (page 60),

MAKES:
One 4" (10cm) pincushion

Those classic tomato pincushions are about as good as it gets when it comes to storing your pins, but it never hurts to have more! My own pincushion collection keeps growing as I keep one for my machine-sewing needles, one for my hand-sewing needles, and one by my machine. Try out your hand-sewing skills on this little guy, and I'm sure he'll find a spot in your sewing home!

Materials

☐ Fat quarter of quilting cotton or 7" x 14" (18 x 35.5cm) remnant of light-to medium-weight woven fabric

☐ Batting

☐ Coordinating embroidery floss

Tools

☐ Basic sewing kit (see page 28)

☐ Embroidery needle

☐ Chopstick or similar turning tool

Your collection of fabric pieces for this project should look something like this:

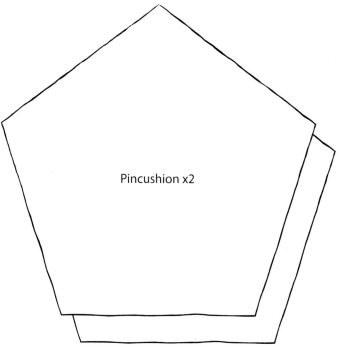

Pincushion x2

THE PREP WORK:
Cut your fabric pieces from the pattern on page 75. Transfer the markings from the pattern onto your fabric.

EMBELLISH IT!
If you'd like to add a button to the center for a special touch, see the feature on buttons on page 106.

TRY OUT HAND SEWING:

Bellflower Pincushion *(continued)*

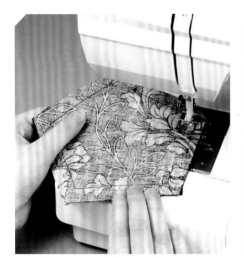

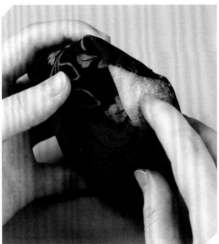

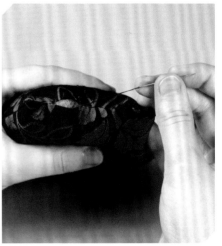

1 **Sew around the pentagon.** Starting and ending where the circles on the pattern indicate for turning the cushion right side out, sew around the perimeter of the pentagon. Trim the seam allowance at the corners and turn the pentagon right side out.

2 **Stuff the cushion.** Poke the corners of the cushion with a chopstick to define them. Using the opening in the side, stuff the cushion lightly with batting, making sure the corners have plenty.

3 **Sew the cushion closed.** Using a ladder stitch, hand sew the opening in the side closed.

Batting

Batting: Pincushions, stuffed animals, pillows—batting stuffs it all!

Batting is the sewing term for stuffing, fluff, or whatever you might call the thing that fills your pillows. It comes in bags of different sizes, but keep in mind that it condenses quite a bit when it has been stuffed properly, so get a bag that's about twice as big as the project you're making. When using batting, be sure to stuff the project a little bit at a time so the end result is smooth and not lumpy.

4 **Sew the center.** With the embroidery floss, sew into the center of the cushion. Loop the needle around the entire cushion, lining up the floss with the pattern markings. Do this with all five lines and sew a knot into the center to complete the cushion.

Pictures in Fabric: Appliqué

Sometimes you can't always find just the fabric you want, or you wish it had a bit of extra oomph! Appliqué embellishments accomplish this perfectly. The name literally comes from the idea of applying one smaller, decorative shape of fabric over another. It's easy to make fantastic-looking designs and pictures with appliqué. It's definitely my favorite kind of embellishment, and with all the designs and options I offer in this book, I hope it will be for you too!

WHY I LOVE APPLIQUÉ, AND YOU SHOULD TOO!

If all the ribbon, rickrack, and lace in the world disappeared tomorrow, I wouldn't be upset one bit as long as I still had my fusible web. I've included loads of appliqué patterns for nearly every project in this book, and here are just some of the reasons why.

Liven up boring fabrics: There are times when you are ready and raring to sew, but the fabric selection at the store just isn't cutting it. Maybe you can't find any prints that you like, or they just don't have the wow factor you're looking for. When you embellish with appliqué, it's like you're making your own fabric design. Even plain, solid fabrics wind up looking amazing!

Use up scraps: Remember when I said you shouldn't throw your fabric scraps away after cutting out your project pieces? Well, here's one way they can be put to good use! Cut all those ragged scraps into beautiful appliqué shapes and pictures.

Customize your look: With all the appliqué patterns there are to choose from in this book, there's bound to be something that catches your eye. Most of the patterns in this book can be used interchangeably, especially if you resize them to your liking. Now when you make your tote bag or book cover, you'll know it's truly your own.

Spruce up a bland project: If you're a little bit past the greenhorn stage of sewing, you might be afraid to jump into complicated patterns, but are a little jaded by beginner projects. Sometimes simple can translate as boring, but this needn't be the case with colorful appliqué! Punch up projects that would otherwise have you yawning with some of your favorite designs in bright colors. It won't be a plain old handmade project anymore!

SUPPLIES

A few helpful supplies can really give you some gorgeous appliqué. Here are some of the materials you might need depending on the look you're going for.

Fusible web: This is similar to the fusible web tape referenced in the Pillow Sham project (page 54); however, there are other kinds of fusible web that come in sheets so they can be applied to large pieces of fabric. It makes appliqué so much easier because it keeps the fabric from shifting while you sew it. Fusible web comes in light adhesive varieties for a temporary hold that will be sewn later, and strong adhesive varieties for a permanent hold that doesn't need to be sewn.

The adhesive works by ironing the fusible side of the paper to the wrong side of your fabric. Once the paper has cooled, peel it off, leaving the adhesive behind. You can then iron the appliqué fabric to your main project, where it will be fused in place by the adhesive.

Fusible web: Sheets of iron-on fusible web come in light- and heavy-duty varieties. You can find them in rolls, by the yard, or as folded sheets.

There are several ways to apply fusible web for the best accuracy and least headache. Here are my favorites.

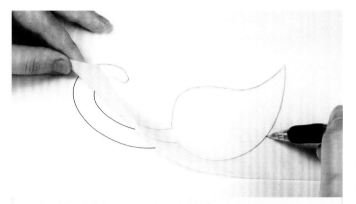

Trace the pattern: Layer the fusible web, adhesive side down, over the pattern page. Trace the pattern shape, and then iron it to your fabric. You can then cut it out, paper and all. This is perfect for patterns that are overlapping. Be warned that this will create a reverse image, so do this only with patterns that can be reversed without affecting the look of the shape.

Outline the pattern: Iron the fusible web to your fabric first, and then outline the cut pattern pieces on the fusible web. This is good for tracing shapes that aren't flat, such as found objects. You can then cut the pieces straight from the fabric and peel away the fusible web paper when ready.

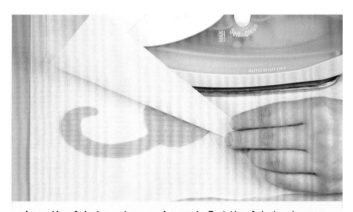

Iron the fabric onto parchment: Cut the fabric shapes from your pattern, and then lay them right side down onto a sheet of parchment paper. Iron the fusible web over the whole sheet and all your pieces will be together until you need them. This is great if you have a lot of pieces to keep track of.

Fabrics: For appliqué fabric choices suitable for beginners, I suggest felt and quilting cotton. Cotton comes in a multitude of colors and is smooth and predictable, but it is also a woven fabric, so it will unravel unless the edges are finished. Felt comes in fewer colors, but being a nonwoven pressed fiber sheet, it does not unravel. Try to find high-quality wool or wool-blend felt, as it lasts much longer and cuts cleaner than its synthetic counterparts.

Felt: Made of mechanically pressed fibers rather than woven or knitted fibers, felt fabrics are categorized as nonwovens.

APPLIQUÉ METHODS

Applying one decorative fabric to another can be done in a number of different ways. You can choose which one you like depending on the difficulty or finished look you are going for. Here are some easy and surefire methods you can try:

Adhesive method

This method uses only fusible web to adhere the appliqué fabric. This is a great simple method for projects that won't receive a lot of washing. After applying the fusible web to your appliqué fabric, iron it to your finished project following the manufacturer's instructions. Just like an iron-on patch, the heavy-duty adhesive will hold the fabric there indefinitely!

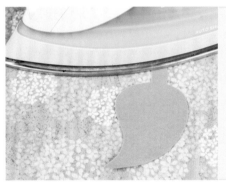

Fusible web:
Heavy-duty

Stitch:
None

Fabric:
Felt

Adhesive method: With just some heavy-duty fusible web, you can iron on any felt appliqué as easily as an iron-on patch.

Floating method

This is what I use to describe the appliqué method in which only a small section of the fabric is sewn down and the rest floats free for a charming three-dimensional effect. Lay your appliqué fabric onto your main fabric and sew it down with a straight stitch along the lines that the pattern indicates, typically along the center of the piece.

Fusible web:
None

Stitch:
Straight

Fabric:
Felt

Floating method: A simple straight stitch down the middle of a felt shape is enough to hold it in place and leaves the rest free for added dimension.

Straight stitch method

With this method, you stitch the edges of your appliqué fabric completely to your main fabric, but you do so easily with just a straight stitch. Use fusible web to adhere your appliqué fabric to the main fabric. Sew along the edge of the appliqué fabric, about ⅛" (0.5cm) in from the edge. See the Sewing Curves feature (page 70) for additional help with this method.

Fusible web:
Light

Stitch:
Straight

Fabric:
Felt

Straight stitch method: Choose a contrasting color thread for a cute shabby-chic look.

Zigzag method

This method takes the longest, but allows you to use cotton as your appliqué fabric without fear of it unraveling. Adhere your appliqué fabric to the main fabric with fusible web. Using a zigzag stitch of short length (0.75–1.25) and medium to wide width (2–4.5), sew along the edges of the appliqué fabric, covering the raw edge of the fabric.

Fusible web:
Light

Stitch:
Zigzag

Fabric:
Felt or cotton

Zigzag method: Use a narrow width zigzag stitch for small appliqué pieces and a wider stitch for larger pieces.

Sweetly Scented Sachet

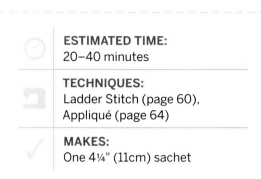

★

ESTIMATED TIME:
20–40 minutes

TECHNIQUES:
Ladder Stitch (page 60),
Appliqué (page 64)

MAKES:
One 4¼" (11cm) sachet

The perfect way to try out your appliqué skills is with this dainty sachet. Fill it with potpourri, herbs, or cedar chips to keep your drawers bug-free and smelling fresh! Choose from a pretty clover, cherry blossom, or wing design for your appliqué piece.

Materials

☐ Fat quarter of quilting cotton or 6" x 12" (15 x 30.5cm) scrap of light- to medium-weight woven fabric, preferably all natural fibers with a loose weave

☐ Fat quarter or 6" x 6" (15 x 15cm) scrap of appliqué fabric (optional)

☐ Fusible web in 6" x 6" (15 x 15cm) square (optional)

☐ Filling (potpourri, dried herbs, or cedar chips)

Tools

☐ Basic sewing kit (see page 28)

☐ Chopstick or similar turning tool

Your collection of fabric pieces for this project should look something like this:

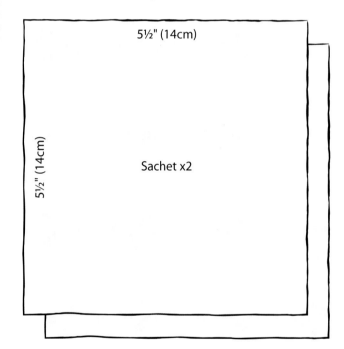

5½" (14cm)

5½" (14cm)

Sachet x2

THE PREP WORK:

Cut your fabric pieces using the following chart, and any appliqué pieces using the patterns on page 75.

Sachet Pieces

Piece Name	Material to Cut	Size to Cut	Number to Cut	Seam Allowance
Sachet	Quilting cotton/lightweight woven	5½" x 5½" (14 x 14cm)	2	⅝" (1.5cm)
Appliqué design (optional)	Appliqué fabric and fusible web	To fit design	1	None

TRY YOUR APPLIQUÉ SKILLS:

Sweetly Scented Sachet (continued)

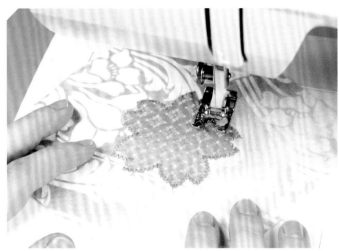

1 **Appliqué your design (optional).** See the appliqué feature on page 64 to choose a method for applying your decorative fabric to your sachet. Sew your appliqué in the center of one of your sachet pieces, or at least 1¼" (3cm) in from the edge of the fabric. Sew the appliqué fabric to the right side of the sachet fabric.

2 **Sew around the perimeter.** Mark a 3" (7.5cm) line along one edge on the wrong side of your sachet fabric, centering it on the edge. This will mark your opening for turning. Place your two pieces of fabric together with right sides facing. Sew around the perimeter of the sachet while skipping over the marked line. Trim the seam allowances at the corners and turn the sachet right side out.

3 **Sew the inner seam.** Poke the corners of the sachet with a chopstick (or similar tool) to define them. Iron the sachet flat. Leaving the same opening as before, sew around the outside of the sachet ¼" (0.5cm) in from the edge.

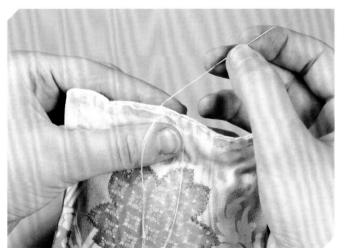

4 **Close the sachet.** Fill the sachet with your selected potpourri, herbs, or cedar chips. Fold in the seam allowances around the opening and sew the inner seam closed with your machine, and the outer seam with a hand-sewn ladder stitch.

Curves Ahead:
Sewing Curves

Many beginners are scared by the idea of sewing curves, but I want you to know that there's nothing to fear! All it takes is a little practice and hand/eye coordination for perfectly smooth and easy curves, but there are some tricks to get you there faster.

Stay in control: Sewing curves might feel unpredictable, so like with any other sewing process that is new to you, give it a try on some scrap fabric. Guide the fabric by lightly pressing with your hands, turning it in one direction or another. Consider sewing like driving a car—slow down on the curves and take it easy; it's on the straight lines that you can go faster. If you need to make the curve especially tight, don't hesitate to stop, lift your presser foot, and turn the fabric to position it where you need it to be. Try sewing several circles or going in a spiral. Start with big loops spanning 12" (30.5cm) pieces of fabric, and then work your way down to smaller 5" (12.5cm) pieces, or pieces that are even smaller.

Seam allowance guides: If you have trouble keeping your seam allowances consistent, seam allowance guides are the perfect help. Store-bought varieties feature a magnet that you can place on your throat plate. When the magnet is adjusted to line up with the right seam allowance, you can butt the edge of your fabric against the magnet while you sew. No matter what kind of crazy curves you're sewing, you're sure to get a perfect seam allowance.

For a quick DIY version, wrap a rubber band around the free arm of your machine. Also try applying layers of masking tape at your seam allowance goal until you reach some height. My favorite quick fix, however, is to use a stack of sticky notes. Peel off only the back note and place the whole block right on your machine. The adhesive is strong, yet temporary, but if it does start to show signs of weakening, peel off the last layer and start fresh!

Sticky notes as seam allowance guides: Probably the easiest and cheapest DIY solution!

CLIPPING CURVES & CORNERS

I briefly mentioned before that when turning a sewn object right side out, you must trim the excess seam allowance fabric to reduce bulk and create crisp corners. The same idea applies when you sew curves.

Clipping concave curves: With curves that sink inward, the resulting turned fabric will be stretched and spread. Concave curves need to have their seam allowances clipped close to the seam without cutting it so the fabric can spread out when it's turned. Take a peek inside and you can see!

Notching convex curves: Give your fabric room to scrunch up by notching it!

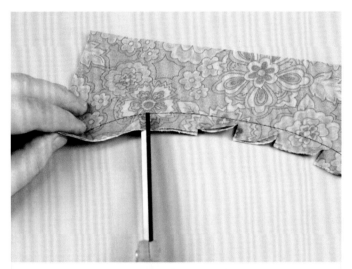

Clipping concave curves: Give your fabric room to spread by clipping it!

Clipping corners: The same ideas apply to convex and concave corners. With corners, the change in angle is more abrupt, so always try to cut as close as you can to the seam without breaking it or weakening it. It helps to back tack several times while sewing the corner to make sure the seam is strong.

Notching convex curves: With curves that bulge outward, the turned fabric will be scrunched together. The excess fabric will cause bulging and your project won't lie flat. Notch the seam allowance fabric close to the seam without cutting it to take out excess fabric. Now your finished seam will have room to move when it's turned. A similar approach is to trim the seam allowance entirely, but be careful, as this can weaken your seam.

Clipping corners: Make your corners crisp and clean by clipping them!

TRY YOUR CURVE-SEWING SKILLS:
Marvelous Mr. & Mrs. Cat

	ESTIMATED TIME:
🕐	45–90 minutes
	TECHNIQUES:
	Appliqué (page 64), Sewing Curves (page 70), Ladder Stitch (page 60)
✓	**MAKES:**
	One 12" (30.5cm)-tall plush animal

*P*ut your curve-sewing skills to the test by making this super-fun stuffed friend! He's covered in adorable appliqué and makes a perfect gift, toy, or decoration. I love using him alongside my throw pillows—it instantly puts a smile on my guests' faces. For the sake of simplicity, he doesn't have a tail, but you can always tell your friends he's a Manx cat!

Materials

- ☐ ½ yd. (50cm) of lightweight woven fabric
- ☐ Fat quarters or 6" x 6" (15 x 15cm) scraps of various appliqué fabrics
- ☐ Fusible web in a 10" x 10" (25.5 x 25.5cm) square
- ☐ Batting

Tools

- ☐ Basic sewing kit (see page 28)
- ☐ Chopstick or similar turning tool

THE PREP WORK:
Cut your fabric and appliqué pieces from the patterns on pages 76–77. Copy any markings from the pattern pieces onto the fabric.

Your collection of fabric pieces for this project should look something like this:

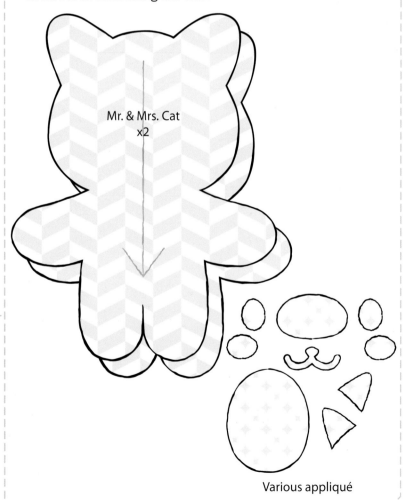

Mr. & Mrs. Cat
x2

Various appliqué

TRY YOUR CURVE-SEWING SKILLS:

Marvelous Mr. & Mrs. Cat *(continued)*

1 **Appliqué your design.** See the appliqué feature (page 64) to choose a method for applying your decorative fabric to the animal front. Sew your appliqué where the pattern guidelines indicate.

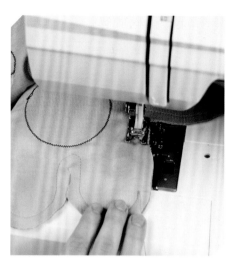

2 **Sew the front to back.** With right sides facing, layer the front and back body pieces together, matching up all the edges. Sew along the perimeter of the pieces, being sure to leave the section between the circles marked on the pattern open for turning right side out. Clip the corners and curves and turn the plush right side out. Use the chopstick to smooth out the curves.

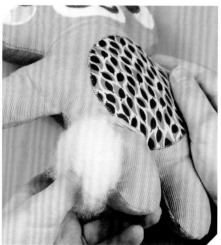

3 **Stuff the plush.** Stuff the plush gradually with batting, first stuffing the arms and legs firmly. Then stuff the ears and head semi-firmly. Stuff the body semi-firmly and the neck lightly. These suggestions are to ensure your plush has a pleasant shape. Either way, be sure your plush is even and full.

4 **Sew the opening closed.** Fold back the seam allowances around the opening and, using a ladder stitch, sew the opening closed.

All Dressed Up!

Does his neck look a little puffy? Cut a 1" x 18" (2.5 x 30.5cm) scrap of felt or fleece (because these fabrics won't unravel). Tie the fabric around your cat's neck like a scarf and cut 1" (2.5cm)-deep and ⅛" (0.5cm)-wide strips of fringe on each end. Now your plushie is one dapper little gent!

Bellflower Pincushion

pages 61–63

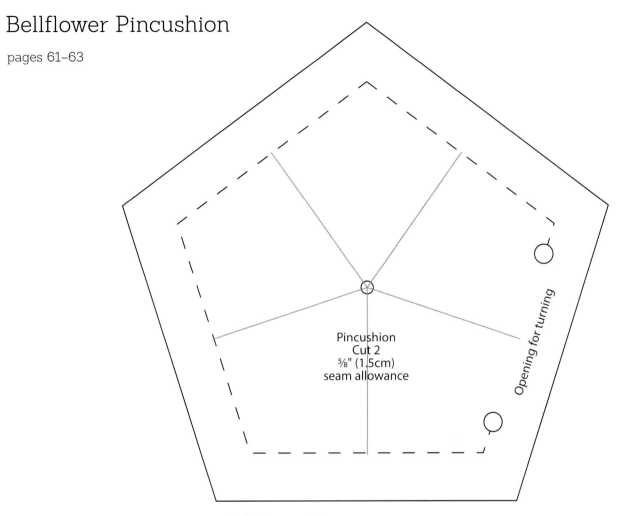

Pincushion
Cut 2
⅝" (1.5cm)
seam allowance

Opening for turning

Enlarge Bellflower Pincushion patterns 125% for actual size.

Sweetly Scented Sachet

pages 67–69

Wing
Appliqué

Clover
Appliqué

Cherry Blossom
Appliqué

Enlarge Sweetly Scented Sachet patterns 125% for actual size.

Marvelous Mr. & Mrs. Cat

pages 72–74

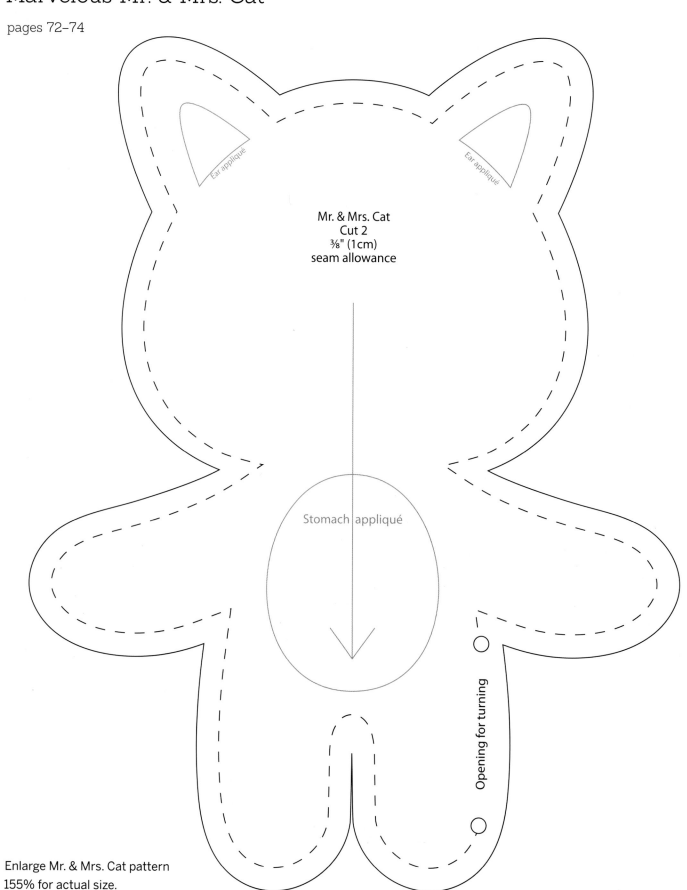

Ear appliqué

Ear appliqué

Mr. & Mrs. Cat
Cut 2
⅜" (1cm)
seam allowance

Stomach appliqué

Opening for turning

Enlarge Mr. & Mrs. Cat pattern
155% for actual size.

Marvelous Mr. & Mrs. Cat (continued)

pages 72–74

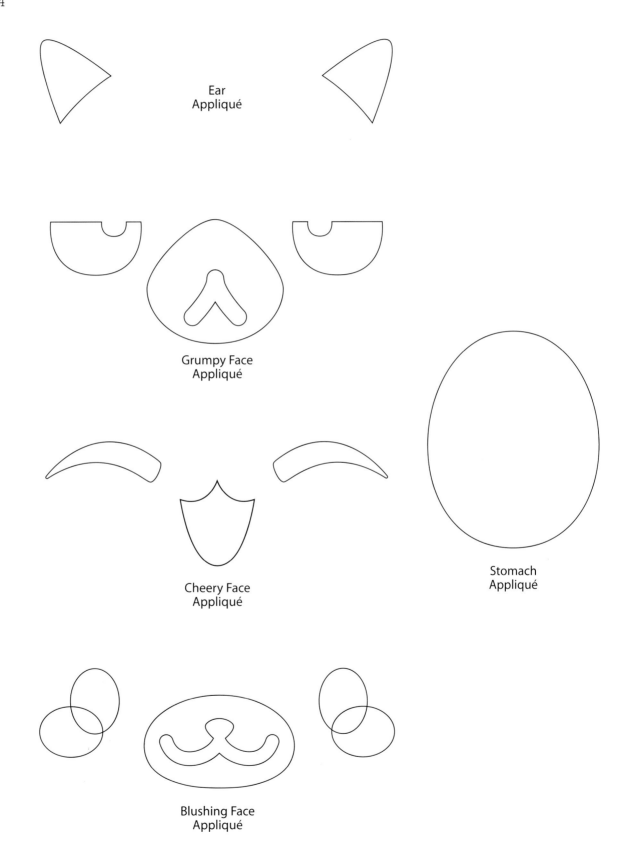

Ear
Appliqué

Grumpy Face
Appliqué

Cheery Face
Appliqué

Stomach
Appliqué

Blushing Face
Appliqué

Enlarge Mr. & Mrs. Cat patterns
155% for actual size.

2

Developing Fabric Skills

In this chapter, you'll learn more about the amazing things you can accomplish with fabric. You can use interfacing to make flimsy fabric sturdy (page 80), make a neat and colorful binding (page 89), or create beautiful ruffles (page 85)! And after you've mastered these skills, you'll have loads of bright and fun projects to use to decorate your home or keep as accessories for yourself. I guarantee that the amazing looks you'll achieve will have you excited for more!

Skills to Master

☐ Interfacing
☐ Gathering Fabric
☐ Binding

82 Chic Placemats

86 Fabric Flower

91 Neat Bound Napkins

Stiff Upper Lip: Interfacing

When shopping for a project, you might find a fabric in a gorgeous print only to discover it is too flimsy and delicate to use for the purpose you had in mind. Or you might finish a project that turns out kind of floppy or lifeless and you wish it had more stability. Interfacing is the answer to these problems. Interfacing is a kind of textile that is used on the inside of projects to give the fabric more stability and rigidity. It's made in a number of different weights that determine how thick and rigid the resulting project will be. Interfacing can be sewn to the fabric to achieve these effects, but more commonly there are iron-on (also known as fusible) varieties that are incredibly easy to use.

Interfacing typically comes in widths of 20" (51cm) or 45" (114.5cm). Projects calling for interfacing will specify these widths when suggesting quantities to purchase. If the width isn't specified then either width is fine.

Varieties: Just like fabric, interfacing comes in a variety of weights and weaves. There are woven interfacings, knit interfacings, and nonwoven interfacings (which are made up of pressed fibers, like felt). Within those categories, they come in different weights, as well as fusible and sew-in varieties. You will likely be limited to the interfacings you can find at your local fabric store, and they will have company names that sometimes do little to describe the interfacing. Your best bet is to get a feel for as many different types of interfacing as you can. Try to find an interfacing with a similar feel to the fabric you're using for the best match. Whether the interfacing is a knit, woven, or nonwoven is fine for these projects, just as long as it has the right weight.

Applying interfacing: I would definitely suggest fusible interfacing for beginner projects, as it is a lot easier to use and work with. However, be sure to test your interfacing on some scrap fabric before you get started. Use a press cloth (like a scrap of plain cotton) to protect the iron from the adhesive during this test run, and follow the manufacturer's instructions to fuse the interfacing to the wrong side of your fabric. Go over each section thoroughly, and then allow the piece to cool completely before checking the corners to see if they adhered.

Interfacing: Go with a fusible interfacing that's just the right weight first, and only worry about whether it's woven, knit, or nonwoven if you're extra finicky.

Ironing interfacing: Let the iron fully heat up each section of the interfacing so the adhesive can melt.

SPECIAL INTERFACINGS

In addition to the typical light-, medium-, and heavyweight varieties of interfacing, you might come across others. They require a bit more practice to work with, but it's good to know they're out there when you're ready for them.

Ultra-firm interfacing: If you find this interfacing in the sewing aisles, it should really stand out to you. It's incredibly firm and practically like fabric cardboard. One version of it is known as Peltex. With the right skills, it can create some really wonderful and sturdy bags, boxes, and other items.

Fusible fleece: This interfacing is soft, thick, and lofted just like fleece, but has adhesive on one side. Apply this type of interfacing to fabrics that need some stability but that you still want to be soft to the touch. Laptop bags would be a good application for this interfacing.

Insulated interfacing: This interfacing has a similar texture to fusible fleece but has an insulated layer, making it perfect for lunch bags and oven mitts. This variety is typically not fusible, but rather a sew-in interfacing. You'll need to baste it to your fabric before continuing with your project.

Pro Tip

Is your interfacing not quite big enough for your project piece? Don't be afraid to overlap and iron several pieces together to get the right coverage. Just try to keep the overlapping to a minimum so the finished product doesn't look bulky. Best of all, because interfacing is always on the inside of the fabric, no one needs to know!

Specialty interfacing: Ultra-firm interfacing, fusible fleece, and insulated interfacing are interesting choices to experiment with when you have more projects under your belt.

Interfacing has a vast range of uses, from making lightweight fabrics more rigid to providing stability for adding embellishments like grommets and eyelets. Ultra-firm interfacing can even be used to give fabric a definitive shape, as was done with these boxes.

TRY YOUR INTERFACING SKILLS:
Chic Placemats

★☆☆☆☆☆☆☆

⏱ **ESTIMATED TIME:**
30–60 minutes

TECHNIQUES:
Ladder Stitch (page 60),
Appliqué (page 64),
Interfacing (page 80)

✓ **MAKES:**
One 14" x 18"
(35.5 x 45.5cm) placemat

A simple rectangle of fabric is transformed into a professional-looking piece of home décor with some interfacing and stylish wave, chevron, or sprout appliqué!

Your collection of fabric pieces for this project should look something like this:

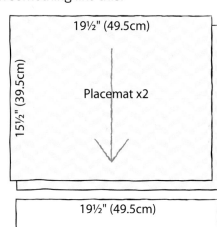

19½" (49.5cm)

15½" (39.5cm)

Placemat x2

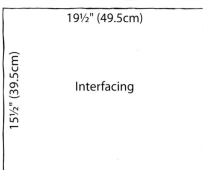

19½" (49.5cm)

15½" (39.5cm)

Interfacing

Materials

☐ ½ yd. (50cm) light- to medium-weight woven fabric

☐ ½ yd. (50cm) lightweight fusible interfacing

☐ Fat quarter of appliqué fabric (optional)

☐ ½ yd. (50cm) fusible web (optional)

Tools

☐ Basic sewing kit (see page 28)

☐ Chopstick or similar turning tool

THE PREP WORK:

Cut your fabric pieces using the following chart, and any appliqué pieces using the patterns on page 93.

Placemat Pieces

Piece Name	Material to Cut	Size to Cut	Number to Cut	Seam Allowance
Placemat	Lightweight woven	19½" x 15½"(49.5 x 39.5cm)	2	⅝" (1.5cm)
Placemat interfacing	Lightweight interfacing	19½" x 15½"(49.5 x 39.5cm)	1	⅝" (1.5cm)
Appliqué design (optional)	Appliqué fabric and fusible web	To fit design	1	None

TRY YOUR INTERFACING SKILLS:

Chic Placemats (continued)

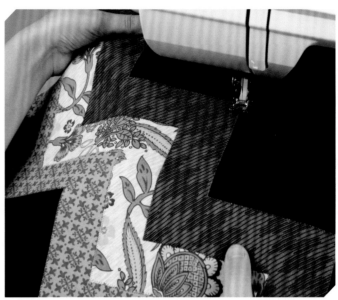

1 **Apply the interfacing.** Line up the interfacing piece over the fabric piece that will be the top of your placemat. Following the manufacturer's directions, fuse the interfacing completely to the wrong side of the fabric.

2 **Appliqué your design (optional).** See the appliqué feature on page 64 to choose a method for applying your decorative fabric to the top of your placemat. Sew your appliqué at least 1" (2.5cm) in from the edge to avoid being cut off, or place it running off the edge for a border look like the chevron or wave patterns.

3 **Sew the perimeter.** Mark a 5" (12.5cm) line along one edge on the wrong side of your placemat fabric, placing it in a spot that has no appliqué. This will mark your opening for turning. Place your two pieces of fabric together with right sides facing. Sew around the entire perimeter of the placemat, skipping over the marked line.

4 **Sew the opening closed.** Clip the corners of the seam allowances, and then turn the placemat right side out. Poke the corners with a chopstick for more definition and press the placemat. Fold under the seam allowances around the opening, and, using a ladder stitch, hand sew the opening closed.

All Ruffled Up:
Gathering Fabric

Have you ever wondered how to make all the fancy ruffles you see in some clothing and home décor items? The truth is, it's quite easy and doesn't take a lot of effort! Here are a few ways to give gathering a shot for some truly gorgeous waves.

Twin seams method: Set your machine to a straight stitch at the longest length you have. Use a lightweight fabric such as quilting cotton. Begin sewing along the edge of your fabric within the seam allowance of your project. Do not back tack or trim your thread tails at the beginning; rather, leave them very long (at least 6" [15cm]). Do, however, back tack

Twin seams gathering: Two rows of very long stitches are all you need to make gathers. This also works with hand stitches!

your seam at the end. Repeat this same stitch again close to the first one, being very careful not to sew over the previous seam. This extra seam is done for insurance while you gather the fabric.

After both rows of stitching are completed, pull the two threads from the bobbin with one hand while pulling the fabric with the other. Start out gently, almost sliding the fabric to the other end of the threads. Be careful not to be too harsh, or you can break both threads and will have to start over. You'll see that the fabric starts to create ruffles. Keep doing this until the fabric ruffles with the look that you want or until it reaches the length you need. Tie the bobbin threads to your top threads to hold the gathers in place temporarily.

Use the gathered fabric with your project as you would any other piece of fabric, but remember that the gathers will continue to shift until your fabric edge is sewn to something else.

Couching method: This is a faster gathering method that's better for thicker or longer lengths of fabric because it's much sturdier. It requires a piece of narrow ribbon or cording (about ⅛" [0.5cm] wide) that is the length of your fabric edge. Begin by laying the ribbon along the edge where you plan to sew, within your seam allowance. Using a very wide zigzag stitch at a medium to long length, sew over the ribbon or cord, making sure it is completely covered but isn't pierced by the needle. Back tack over the ribbon at the end of your seam as in the twin seams method. When you finish, the ribbon or cord should move freely underneath the thread, as if the thread has created a kind of casing or channel.

Pull at the ribbon or cord the same as with the bobbin threads in the previous method. You'll begin to develop gathers and there will be less of a chance of thread breakage.

Making the gathers: Hold the bobbin threads with one hand while gently sliding the fabric down the threads with the other.

Couching method: Set your zigzag stitch as wide as you can to make sure it goes over the ribbon completely.

TRY YOUR GATHERING SKILLS:
Fabric Flower

★☆☆☆☆☆☆☆

ESTIMATED TIME:
15–30 minutes

TECHNIQUES:
Gathering (page 85),
Hand Sewing (page 58)

MAKES:
One 2" (5cm) flower

A perfect way to test your gathering skills is to make this fabric flower. With nothing but a simple strip of fabric, you'll have a wonderful embellishment that can be hand sewn anywhere!

Materials

☐ ⅛ yd. (12.5cm) of lightweight woven fabric

Tools

☐ Basic sewing kit (see page 28)

Your collection of fabric pieces for this project should look something like this:

	18" (45.5cm)
3" (7.5cm)	Fabric Flower

THE PREP WORK:
Cut an 18" x 3" (45.5 x 7.5cm) strip of fabric.

When added to a floral print, these flowers can give your fabric a three-dimensional look!

TRY YOUR GATHERING SKILLS:

Fabric Flower (continued)

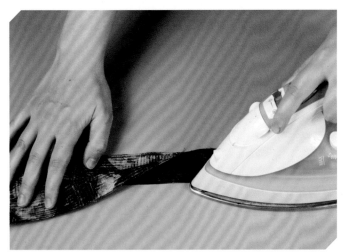

1 **Fold the fabric.** Fold the fabric in half lengthwise with wrong sides together and iron it flat.

2 **Sew the gathering stitches.** Using a gathering stitch, sew two rows of stitches completely around the raw open edges of the rectangle: the side, bottom, and then the other side. Do not sew the folded side.

3 **Gather the fabric.** Begin gathering the fabric as described in the gathering feature on page 85. Stop when the fabric measures 6" (15cm) long.

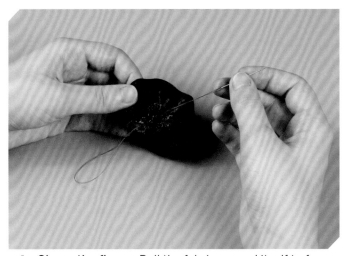

4 **Shape the flower.** Roll the fabric around itself to form a pinwheel and make the flower shape. Hand sew several knots that wrap around the bottom of the flower to hold the gathers in place. Hand sew this to any project for a beautiful embellishment!

Even Easier!
Try this with ribbon and you won't have to worry about raw edges!

Bound with Style: Binding

Like hemming and pinking, binding is another way of finishing edges, but it does so with much more style. Because you're wrapping a raw edge with another fabric, you can choose whatever fabric you want for a snazzy contrast. For a beginner's introduction, we'll be applying a mitered binding made from vertical and horizontal strips of your favorite fabric. It takes some time to get used to, but once you understand the concept you'll be surprised how easy it is!

1 **Make one long strip.** Your pattern will indicate how long and wide your binding needs to be. Because it needs to be one continuous strip to cover your entire project edge, there's a good chance you won't have enough fabric to make the full length. To connect your pieces to make one long strip, line up the corners of the ends so they are at a 90° angle. Draw a line connecting the upper left corner to the lower right corner.

2 **Chain the pieces.** Sew along this line to create a diagonal connection between strips. Sewing diagonally makes a nice smooth seam that will be less bulky on your finished project than if you had connected the edges vertically. Trim away the excess fabric and press the seam open.

3 **Iron the binding.** Fold the binding in half lengthwise with wrong sides together, matching the raw edges. Iron the entire piece flat.

4 **Begin the binding.** Measure 6" (15cm) down from the end of your binding fabric and match up this point with the center of one of your project edges. Line up the raw edge of the binding with the edge of your project from the right side. Begin sewing from the middle of the project edge, using the suggested seam allowance.

5 **Begin the corner.** When you come to a corner, stop before you get to the edge at a distance equal to your seam allowance. Pivot your work and sew off the edge of your project at a diagonal.

6 **Finish the corner.** Fold your binding back at a diagonal, away from your project, then fold it back toward your project, lining up the raw edge of your binding with the edge of your project as before.

7 **Continue attaching the binding.** Prepare to sew the next side. Start your seam at the very end of the fabric and back tack frequently so the seam is strong. Continue attaching the binding along the new side. Repeat steps 5–7 to create the other corners and sew the remaining sides.

8 **Connect the ends.** Stop about 6" (15cm) before you reach your ending point. Open up the binding folds and continue to place the binding along the edge of your project until the two binding ends meet. Mark this point, and then sew the two binding ends together along this line with right sides facing. Trim the seam allowance and press the seam open.

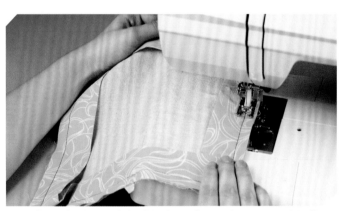

9 **Sew the last of the binding.** Smooth out your binding so the remaining unsewn edge lines up with the edge of your project. Sew this opening to complete the circle. Iron the binding away from the project.

10 **Wrap the binding.** Wrap the binding around the edge of your project toward the back side and fold the corners like you are wrapping a present. Pin and iron the binding in place.

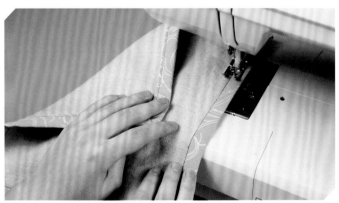

11 **Sew the binding in place.** From the right side of the project, stitch along the line of the previous seam. Your stitching will be less obtrusive and, if done properly, it should catch the edge of the binding from the other side. Flip your work often to make sure this is happening.

TRY YOUR BINDING SKILLS:
Neat Bound Napkins

ESTIMATED TIME:
30 minutes

TECHNIQUES:
Binding (page 89),
Appliqué (page 64)

MAKES:
One 18" (45.5cm) napkin

Test your binding skills by making this super easy bound napkin. The contrast edge and included fan, flower, and leaf appliqué really put a spin on your dining area and make a charming statement!

Materials

☐ ½ yd. (50cm) of handkerchief linen for napkin

☐ ¼ yd. (25cm) of lightweight woven for binding

☐ Fat quarter or 6" x 6" (15 x 15cm) scrap of appliqué fabric (optional)

☐ Fusible web in 6" x 6" (15 x 15cm) square (optional)

Tools

☐ Basic sewing kit (see page 28)

Your collection of fabric pieces for this project should look something like this:

18" (45.5cm)

18" (45.5cm)

Napkin

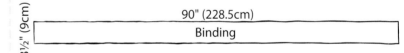

3½" (9cm)

90" (228.5cm)

Binding

THE PREP WORK:

Cut your fabric pieces using the following chart, and any appliqué pieces using the patterns on page 93.

Napkin Pieces

Piece Name	Material to Cut	Size to Cut	Number to Cut	Seam Allowance
Napkin	Handkerchief linen	18" x 18"(45.5 x 45.5cm)	1	None
Binding	Lightweight woven	3½" x 90"(9 x 228.5cm)	1	½" (1.5cm)
Appliqué design (optional)	Appliqué fabric and fusible web	To fit design	1	None

1 **Apply the binding.** Following the binding feature (page 89), prepare your binding and apply it around the edges of your napkin fabric.

2 **Appliqué your design (optional).** See the appliqué feature on page 64 to choose a method for applying your decorative fabric to the napkin front. Sew your appliqué in the center or at least 1" (2.5cm) from the edge of the fabric.

Chic Placemats

pages 82–84

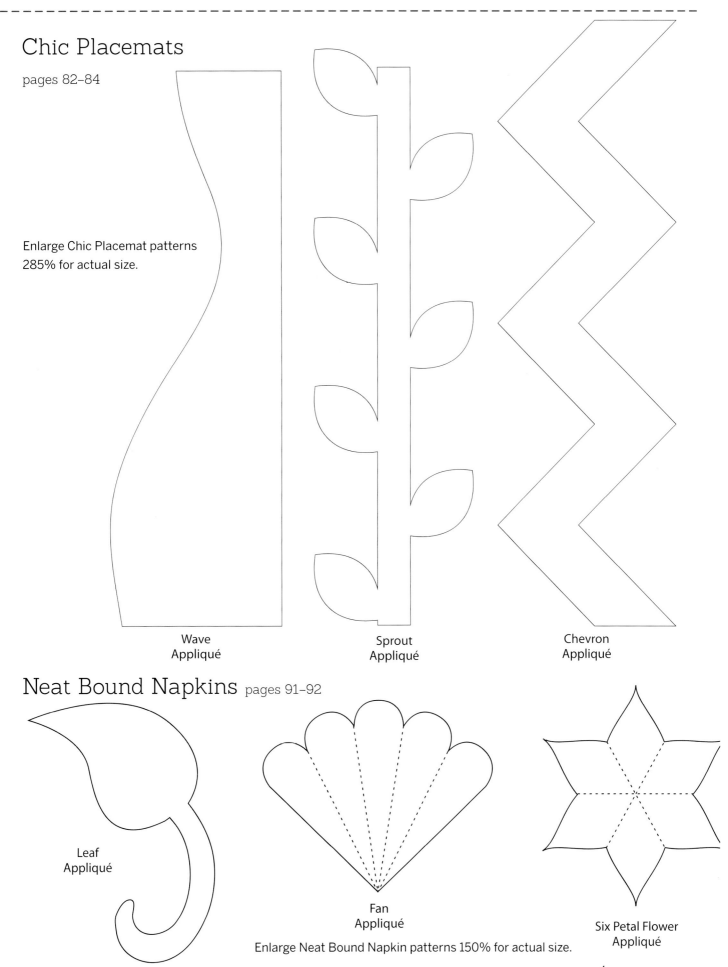

Enlarge Chic Placemat patterns 285% for actual size.

Wave
Appliqué

Sprout
Appliqué

Chevron
Appliqué

Neat Bound Napkins pages 91–92

Leaf
Appliqué

Fan
Appliqué

Six Petal Flower
Appliqué

Enlarge Neat Bound Napkin patterns 150% for actual size.

3

Adding Notions & Closures

This chapter covers all the bits and bobs you can find along with fabric at your local craft store. Specifically we're talking about closures. These are the handy things you can add to your projects so you can open them and close them when you want. You'll be able to see all the options available to you to get the exact look and product you're going for, whether it be a casual and easy look, or something finished and sophisticated. You can make a load of helpful accessories like a wallet or a holder for an MP3 player—perfect for gifts or for yourself. And your knowledge of closures will make the results that much more sophisticated!

Skills to Master

- ☐ Hook-and-Loop Tape
- ☐ Installing Snaps
- ☐ Buttons & Buttonholes
- ☐ Zippers
- ☐ Grommets & Eyelets

97 Belt Loop MP3 Player Holder

102 In-a-Snap Wallet

110 Handy Hand Towels

116 Quick Zip Pouch

121 Convenient Coin Pouch

Fuss-Free Fastening: Hook-and-Loop Tape

We're all familiar with hook-and-loop tape. It's the fuzzy and scratchy stuff that held our shoes together when we were kids. It's also a very simple way of holding parts of your sewing projects closed. It looks best on casual projects or items you need to close up with only one hand, as buttons and snaps often need a two-handed approach.

Varieties: The selection of hook-and-loop tape is somewhat limited. The colors are typically the most basic and the shapes tend to be small. It comes in coin shapes, strips, and tabs. It also comes in heavy-duty adhesive, lightweight adhesive, and sew-in varieties. The adhesive varieties are great for emergencies and bits of help around the house, but stick with the sew-in varieties for the projects in this book for the best results.

Applying hook-and-loop tape: As you can feel, there is a hook side (scratchy side) and a loop side (fluffy side) to hook-and-loop tape, and it's good to be aware of that when placing your pieces. In any project, there will usually be a side that's facing upward and another facing downward. Try to use the fluffy side on the part that's facing upward to avoid undue scratches. The part facing downward should have the scratchy side so it will be less likely to rub against your skin or hurt someone.

Applying hook-and-loop tape: Apply the hook-and-loop tape with sewing pins or even a bit of fusible web tape if you find it keeps shifting.

Sewing hook-and-loop tape: To sew the hook-and-loop tape, use a basic medium-length straight stitch close to the edge of the tape piece (about ⅛" [0.5cm]).

Belt Loop MP3 Player Holder

 ★ ★

⏱ **ESTIMATED TIME:**
20–40 minutes

▣ **TECHNIQUES:**
Hook-and-Loop Tape (page 96)

✓ **MAKES:**
One 2" x 4" (5 x 10cm)
MP3 player holder

Test your hook-and-loop tape skills by making this quick and easy holder for your MP3 player. It goes right over your belt, backpack strap, or other loop and attaches securely for those times when you want your MP3 player in easy reach.

Materials

☐ ¼ yd. (25cm) light- to medium-weight woven fabric

☐ ¾" (2cm) tab of hook-and-loop tape

Tools

☐ Basic sewing kit (see page 28)

☐ Chopstick or similar turning tool

Your collection of fabric pieces for this project should look something like this:

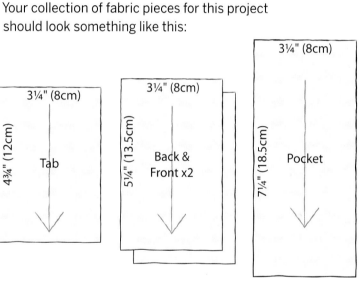

Tab — 3¼" (8cm) x 4¾" (12cm)

Back & Front x2 — 3¼" (8cm) x 5¼" (13.5cm)

Pocket — 3¼" (8cm) x 7¼" (18.5cm)

THE PREP WORK:

Cut your fabric pieces using the following chart:

MP3 Player Holder Pieces

Piece Name	Material to Cut	Size to Cut	Number to Cut	Seam Allowance
Holder back and front	Light- to medium-weight woven	3¼" x 5¼"(8 x 13.5cm)	2	⅝" (1.5cm)
Pocket	Light- to medium-weight woven	3¼" x 7¼"(8 x 18.5cm)	1	⅝" (1.5cm)
Tab	Light- to medium-weight woven	3¼" x 4¾"(8 x 12cm)	1	⅝" (1.5cm)

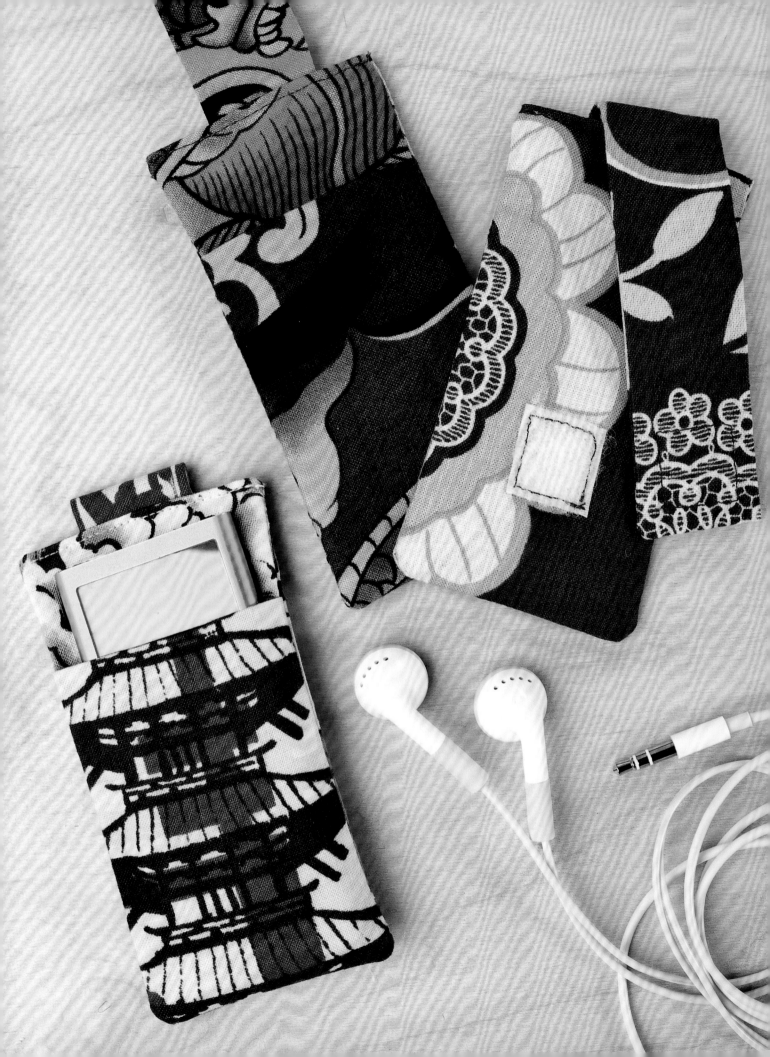

TRY YOUR HOOK-AND-LOOP TAPE SKILLS:

Belt Loop MP3 Player Holder *(continued)*

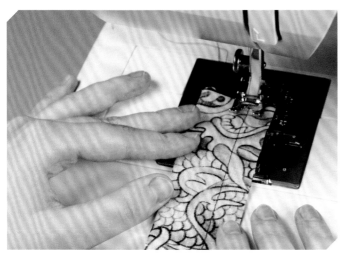

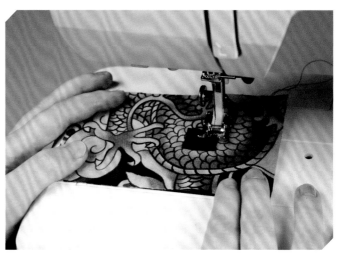

1 **Sew the tab.** Fold the tab piece in half lengthwise with right sides together and sew along the open long side and one short side on the bottom. The top should be left free for turning right side out. Clip the seam allowances, turn the tab right side out with a chopstick, and iron the piece flat.

2 **Apply the hook-and-loop tape.** Take a piece of hook-and-loop tape and center the hooked side on the bottom sewn end of the tab. Sew it in place following the hook-and-loop tape feature (page 96) for extra help. Apply the loop side 3" (7.5cm) down from the top of the holder back on the right side, centering it horizontally.

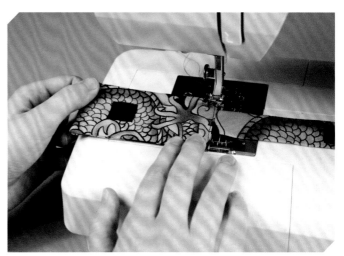

3 **Sew the pocket to the back.** Fold the pocket in half widthwise with wrong sides together, lining up the raw edges. Line the open edge of the folded pocket against the bottom edge of the holder back on the right side of the fabric. Layer the holder front on top so the right sides of the two holder pieces are facing. Sew around every edge except the top. Trim the seam allowances, turn the holder right side out, and press. Flip the pocket so that the hook-and-loop tape is on the opposite side.

4 **Attach the tab.** Tuck the seam allowances into the top of the holder and press. With the hook-and-loop pieces both facing up, slip the tab into the top and sew across the top edge, close to the folds.

Looking Snappy: Installing Snaps

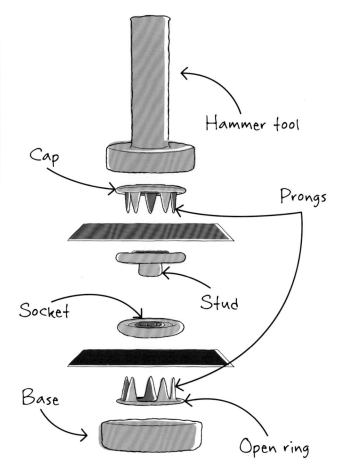

Hammer tool

Cap

Prongs

Socket

Stud

Base

Open ring

Anatomy of a snap: To ensure proper installation, prong snaps should be hammered in a specific order.

Snaps are another great closure to tie up your latest project. The sew-in variety is extremely dainty and unobtrusive—perfect if you want a completely inconspicuous closure. If you go with the prong variety, they look quite classy and have a much stronger hold than hook-and-loop tape.

Varieties of snaps: Sew-in snaps vary in size from very dainty sizes at ¼" (0.5cm) in diameter up to large 1" (2.5cm)-diameter sizes. Prong snaps are typically made from various colors of metal but can also vary in size. The actual cap of the snap can be decorative or plain, but the construction is almost always the same.

Setting sew-in snaps: Sew-in snaps typically have several holes on the sides that allow you to anchor the snap to your project with your thread. Place the stud end of your snap on the part of the project that will be facing downward, where the pattern indicates. Sew it in place and prepare to sew the socket piece.

You can mark the end of the stud with your fabric marker or a bit of chalk, and then rub the stud onto the fabric of your project. This is where you can install your socket piece. The pattern may also indicate where to sew your snap socket, but this can serve as an insurance policy. Repeat the same process for sewing the socket part of the snap as you did for the stud.

Setting prong snaps: Prong snaps are much stronger than sew-in snaps because they're held together with hooked metal. Your fabric should be reinforced with interfacing whenever possible if you'll be installing prong snaps.

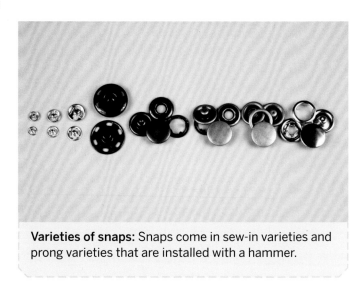

Varieties of snaps: Snaps come in sew-in varieties and prong varieties that are installed with a hammer.

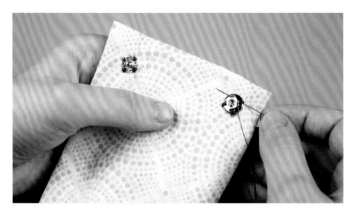

Sew-in snaps: Anchor the sew-in snaps to your project with several stitches around the holes in the snap—about three to five. Slip the needle between the layers of the fabric toward the next hole and repeat the process until you've sewn all the way around.

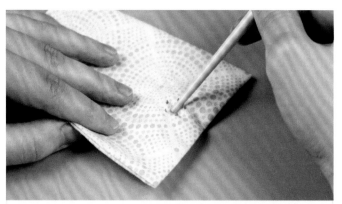

Prong snaps: Insert the snap cap. Find and mark the area where the snap needs to be installed. From the underside, poke the prongs through the fabric so they're visible on the other side. Use a pencil or similar tool to poke into the center and force the prongs to come through.

Completing the snap: When you've finished hammering your prong snap, be sure that the pieces have no space between them and are completely joined. If you pull at it lightly, the snap should not give. If the join isn't strong, it's best to pull the snaps apart with pliers, straighten out the prongs, and try again. Repeat this same process with the snap ring that serves as the next prong piece plus the socket piece. This part should be installed on your project so the ring faces inward.

Troubleshooting: Sometimes no matter what you try, you can't get the prongs to make a strong enough join. Perhaps when the snap is closed you can't open it again without ripping it out of the fabric. I've had this issue many times before, and this can result from the stud and socket being off in size by a bit. To solve this problem, I found that putting a dab of multi-purpose craft glue on your fabric before setting the snap works wonders. You must make sure the glue dries completely before you attempt to open and close the snap again, but it's a great insurance policy against snaps that are too tight!

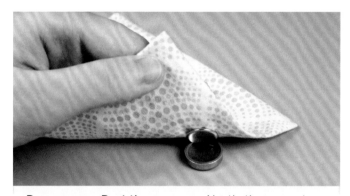

Prong snaps: Rest the snap cap. Nestle the cap onto your setting tool. You should feel it rest there easily so that it won't move while it's hammered.

Prong snaps: Hammer the snap. Set the snap socket piece on top of the prongs. You should feel it rest in the grooves. When you know that it feels settled, set your hammering tool on top of the socket and hammer it well. When the snap is hammered, the prongs of the snap cap are forced backward and into the grooves of the socket when the hammer tool strikes them.

TRY YOUR SNAP-INSTALLING SKILLS:
In-a-Snap Wallet

★ ★ ★ ☆ ☆ ☆ ☆ ☆

ESTIMATED TIME:
45–90 minutes

TECHNIQUES:
Snap Installation (page 100),
Interfacing (page 80),
Appliqué (page 64),
Sewing Curves (page 70)

MAKES:
One 3¾" x 2¾" (9.5 x 7cm)
tri-fold wallet

Test your skills at applying snaps with this handy little wallet. It's perfect for holding a few credit cards or some spare bills and it's not too fussy or big to be slipped into your pocket! The long shape makes it perfect for repeating appliqué motifs, like the included teardrop, hexagon, or cube shapes.

Materials

☐ ¼ yd. (25cm) of lightweight woven fabric

☐ ¼ yd. (25cm) of lightweight interfacing

☐ One sew-in or metal prong snap about ¼"–¾" (0.6–1.9cm) in diameter

☐ Fat quarter or 6" x 6" (15 x 15cm) scrap of appliqué fabric (optional)

☐ 6" x 6" (15x 15cm) square of fusible web (optional)

Tools

☐ Basic sewing kit (see page 28)

☐ Snap setting tools (if applicable)

☐ Chopstick or similar turning tool

Your collection of fabric pieces for this project should look something like this:

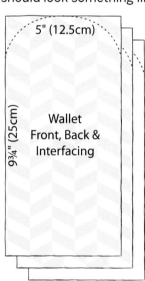

5" (12.5cm)

9¾" (25cm)

Wallet
Front, Back &
Interfacing

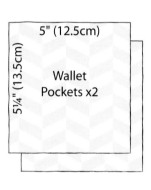

5" (12.5cm)

5¼" (13.5cm)

Wallet
Pockets x2

THE PREP WORK:

Cut your fabric pieces using the following chart, and any appliqué pieces using the patterns on page 124.

Wallet Pieces

Piece Name	Material to Cut	Size to Cut	Number to Cut	Seam Allowance
Wallet	Lightweight woven	5" x 9¾"(12.5 x 25cm)	2	⅝" (1.5cm)
Wallet interfacing	Lightweight interfacing	5" x 9¾"(12.5 x 25cm)	1	⅝" (1.5cm)
Pockets	Lightweight woven	5" x 5¼"(12.5 x 13.5cm)	2	⅝" (1.5cm)
Appliqué design (optional)	Appliqué fabric and fusible web	To fit design	1	None

In-a-Snap Wallet (continued)

1 **Apply the interfacing.** Pick the piece of fabric you'd like to use for the outside of your wallet. Line up the wallet interfacing over the wrong side of the wallet fabric. Following the manufacturer's directions, fuse it to the wrong side of the fabric completely.

2 **Trim the wallet edge.** Using a soup can, cup, or similar round edge, trace a semicircle on one end of your wallet front and back pieces and trim them so the end is rounded instead of square. This will be the flap of your wallet.

3 **Appliqué your design (optional).** See the appliqué feature on page 64 to choose a method for applying your decorative fabric to the wallet piece with interfacing applied. Sew your appliqué on the center of the wallet or at least 1" (2.5cm) from the edge of the fabric so it won't be cut off.

4 **Prepare the pockets.** Take one pocket piece and fold it in half widthwise with right sides together. Sew along the open long edge. Turn the pocket right side out and press the seam. Repeat with the second pocket piece, folding it in the same manner, but with wrong sides facing. Iron it flat, and do not stitch it.

5 **Apply the middle pocket.** Take the wallet piece without the interfacing applied. Mark a horizontal line across the right side 3⅝" (9cm) up from the bottom (non-curved) edge. This is your pocket placement line. Align the sewn edge of your first pocket with this line, facing the folded edge of the pocket toward the top curved end of the wallet. Stitch the bottom edge of the pocket in place.

TRY YOUR SNAP-INSTALLING SKILLS:
In-a-Snap Wallet *(continued)*

6 **Baste the pockets.** Align the raw edge of the remaining pocket with the bottom edge of the wallet, lining up the raw edges. Baste within the seam allowances of the wallet to hold the sides and bottom of the bottom pocket and the sides of the middle pocket in place.

7 **Sew the wallet.** Place the two wallet pieces together with right sides facing. Mark a 4" (10cm) line centered along one long edge of the wallet. This will be your opening for turning, and it will have to pass over your middle pocket. Sew entirely around the wallet edges, skipping over this line. Trim the seam allowances, turn the wallet right side out, define the corners with a chopstick, and press the seams.

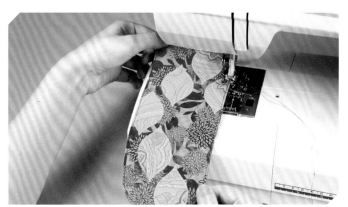

8 **Edge stitch the wallet.** Tuck in the seam allowances around the opening and press them flat. Edge stitch about ⅛" (0.5cm) around the perimeter of the wallet, closing up the opening.

9 **Install the snaps.** Fold the wallet in thirds to find where you'd like to sew the snap. Use the snaps feature (page 100) for help with this. Mine is placed ⅜" (1cm) from the top edge of the wallet, but it can vary based on the thickness of your fabric.

A Spectacular Surprise!
Dress this up in your gift recipient's favorite fabrics and colors and this makes one perfect gift card holder!

Cute as a Button: Buttons & Buttonholes

Buttons and buttonholes are yet another kind of closure that can be used in accessories or clothing. They are perfect if you want to show off a decorative button, but I think their best attribute is that they are less likely to scratch or poke you when you least expect it like zippers, hook-and-loop tape, or snaps might do.

Sewing a buttonhole: A buttonhole is essentially a square of tight zigzag stitches with a hole cut in the center for the button to slip through. The zigzag stitches prevent the cut edges from unraveling. If you have a sewing machine with a buttonhole function, a precise square is very easy to make, but here are some pointers to make sure you understand how your machine does it.

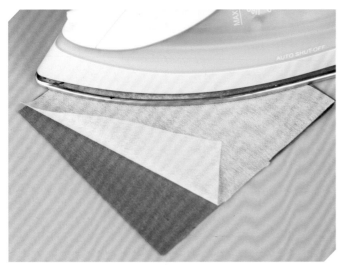

1 **Apply interfacing.** Buttonholes should be stabilized with interfacing so the dense stitches don't warp the fabric. Apply the selected interfacing to the wrong side of your fabric before sewing the buttonholes.

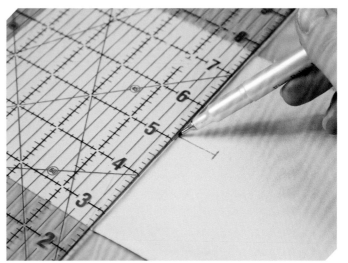

2 **Mark your buttonholes.** Accurately mark your pattern for where your buttonhole should go. Your lines should be equal to the diameter of your button plus ⅛" (0.5cm) for extra moving room. If your button is ball-shaped or particularly tall, add the height of the button as well. Mark two ¼" (0.5cm) perpendicular lines at the end of the buttonhole guide; this will give you extra guidance for making the buttonhole a square.

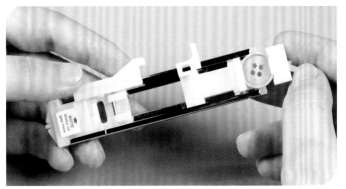

3 **For a one-step buttonhole machine: Prepare the button foot.** If your machine offers a one-step buttonhole function, it won't work properly unless you use the available buttonhole foot to measure your button. If yours is lost, you can usually order a replacement online.

4 **For a one-step buttonhole machine: Sew the buttonhole.** Install your buttonhole presser foot with the button loaded into the back. Check your manufacturer's instructions, as you might have to engage a buttonhole guide for this stitch. When you choose the buttonhole stitch from your machine, it should create the entire buttonhole when you press down the foot pedal until it finishes.

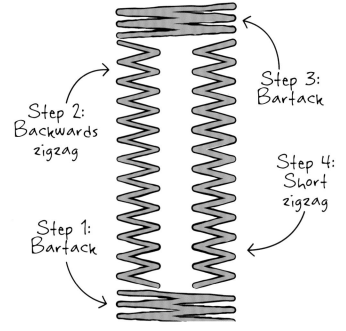

Step 2: Backwards zigzag

Step 3: Bartack

Step 4: Short zigzag

Step 1: Bartack

Four-step buttonhole: A four-step buttonhole machine will usually follow these steps to create the buttonhole.

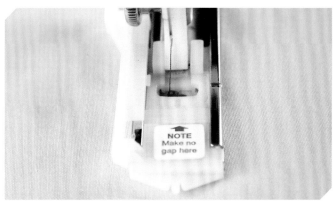

5 **For a four-step buttonhole machine: Start the buttonhole.** Set your stitch length to very short, usually 0.5. Line up your presser foot so the needle will begin sewing to the bottom left of your center line. Select step 1, which will sew the bottom side.

6 **For a four-step buttonhole machine: Complete the buttonhole.** Select step 2, which will sew the left side of the buttonhole going backward. Step 3 will sew the top of your buttonhole. Finally, step 4 forms the right side and completes the buttonhole.

7 **For a freehand buttonhole: Sew the top side.**
If for some reason you have a much older machine without a buttonhole stitch, you can still make one from scratch! It takes more precision but isn't impossible. First, set your machine to a zigzag stitch at 0.5 length and very wide (around 4–5). Sew a short bar of stitches, called a bartack, about ⅛" (0.3cm) along your top guideline.

8 **For a freehand buttonhole: Sew the right side.** Adjust your stitch width to very narrow, around 1–2, and reposition your needle so the right edge of the zigzag aligns with the right edge of your top edge. Sew all the way down to the bottom guideline.

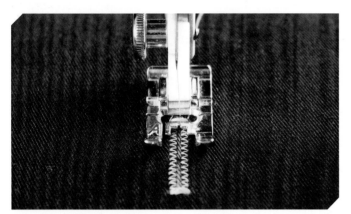

9 **For a freehand buttonhole: Complete the buttonhole.**
Move your needle back to the top so the left edges match up and sew the left side. Repeat Step 7 to sew the bottom edge.

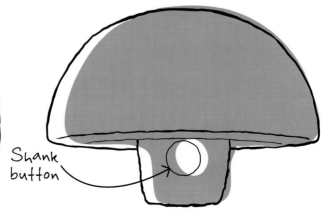

10 **For all buttonholes: Cut the center.** Using a seam ripper or very tiny and sharp scissors, cut the center of your buttonhole without clipping any of your stitches.

Sewing a button: Even non-sewers should know this technique—you can save dozens of shirts just by knowing how to reattach a lost button!

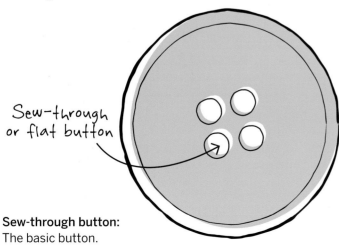

Sew-through or flat button

Sew-through button:
The basic button.

Shank button

Shank button: This rounded button already has a shank, so you can skip Step 5 on the next page.

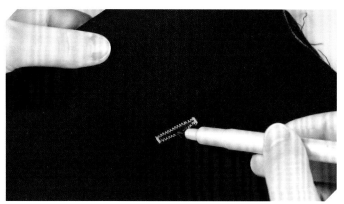

1 **Mark your placement.** Lay your finished buttonhole over the fabric where you expect the button to lie so the project looks right. Mark a dot in the center of the buttonhole to get accurate placement.

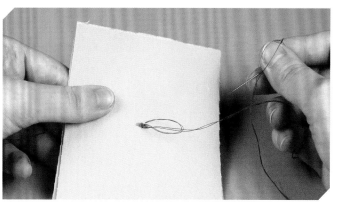

2 **Create a knot.** Prepare your needle and thread as if you were going to hand sew, creating a knot in the fabric; see the Hand Sewing feature (page 58) for more help with this. Make the knot with your thread on the place you marked.

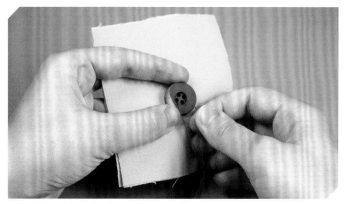

3 **Place the button.** Thread the needle through one hole in the button and hold the button in place on the fabric. Bring the needle down through the opposite buttonhole and the fabric.

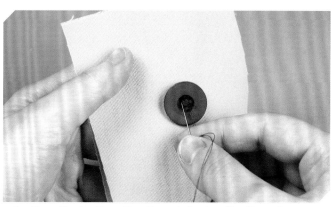

4 **Sew the button.** Continue bringing the thread up through the original buttonhole and back down into the opposite hole until the attachment feels secure (about five times). Repeat with any remaining buttonholes.

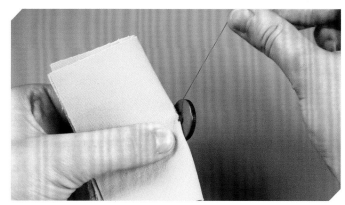

5 **Make the shank.** Bring the thread up through the fabric, but not the button. Instead, tilt the button and bring the needle out from underneath it. Wrap the thread around the stitches you've made about five times to create a shank. This creates some space between the fabric and the button. Create a knot in your fabric and clip the threads off to finish, just as in hand sewing (see page 58).

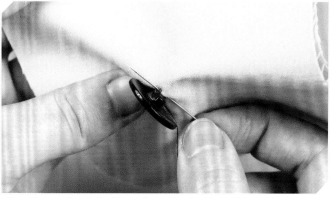

6 **For a shank button: Sew the button.** Work through Step 2 above the same as with a flat button. Instead of sewing through several buttonholes, however, continually sew through the shank in the button, and then through the fabric until the button is secure. Step 5 can be skipped because a shank is built into the button.

TRY YOUR BUTTON-ATTACHING SKILLS:

Handy Hand Towels

★ ★ ★ ☆ ☆ ☆ ☆

 ESTIMATED TIME:
30–60 minutes

TECHNIQUES:
Buttons & Buttonholes
(page 106),
Hemming (page 53)

MAKES:
One hanging tab for a standard-size kitchen hand towel

Test your button-working skills by adding a handy loop to a favorite hand towel. Now you know it will stay put where you need it in addition to looking amazing!

Materials

- ☐ ⅛ yd. (12.5cm) of lightweight woven fabric
- ☐ ⅛ yd. (12.5cm) of lightweight fusible interfacing
- ☐ One hand towel, at least 6" (15cm) wide
- ☐ One button about ½"–1" (1.3–2.5cm) in diameter

Tools

- ☐ Basic sewing kit (see page 28)
- ☐ Chopstick or similar turning tool

Your collection of fabric pieces for this project should look something like this:

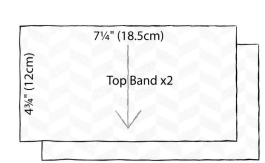

THE PREP WORK:

Cut your fabric pieces using the following chart:

Hand Towel Pieces

Piece Name	Material to Cut	Size to Cut	Number to Cut	Seam Allowance
Tab	Lightweight woven and interfacing	4" x 10"(10 x 25.5cm)	1 of each material	⅝" (1.5cm)
Top band	Lightweight woven	7¼" x 4¾"(18.5 x 12cm)	2	⅝" (1.5cm)

TRY YOUR BUTTON-ATTACHING SKILLS:

Handy Hand Towels (continued)

1 **Apply the interfacing.** Line up the corresponding interfacing piece over the tab piece. Following the manufacturer's directions, fuse it to the wrong side of the fabric completely.

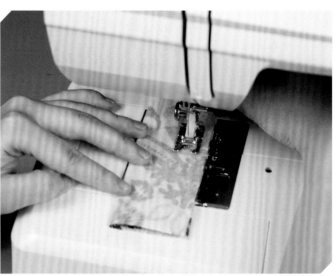

2 **Sew the tab.** Fold the tab piece in half lengthwise with right sides together. Sew along the open long edge and the short bottom edge, leaving the top free for turning right side out. Trim the seam allowances, turn the tab right side out, define the corners with a chopstick, and press the seam.

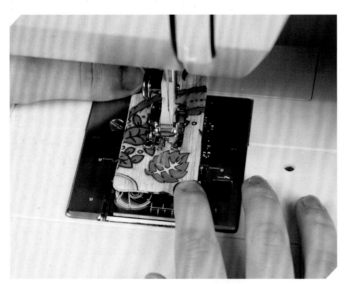

3 **Sew the buttonhole.** Sew the buttonhole for your button, centering it on the finished end of the tab. See the buttonhole feature on page 106 for more help.

4 **Sew the top band.** Layer the two top band pieces together with right sides facing. Insert the unfinished end of the tab piece in between them on one of the long sides, lining up the raw edges. Center the tab along the long side and sew all the layers together along that side only. Finish and press the seam.

TRY YOUR BUTTON-ATTACHING SKILLS:

Handy Hand Towels (continued)

5 **Fold the towel.** Fold your chosen towel so the upper edge is 6" (15cm) across. Fold the towel to the length you want for the finished project. Iron the folds in place in preparation for sewing.

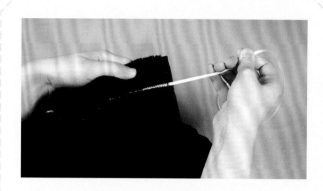

Frilly & Fancy!
Instead of folding your towel in Step 5, consider gathering it using the couching method!

6 **Hem the sides.** Fold over the sides of the top band by ⅝" (1.5cm), or adjust your hems accordingly so the top band is as wide as your folded towel. Iron the folds in place and sew along the raw edges to create single-fold hems.

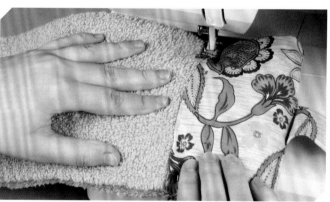

7 **Apply the top band.** Fold under the bottom and top edges of the top band by ⅝" (1.5cm) and iron the folds in place. Nestle the top band around the fold of your towel so that the folded edges of the top band match up on each side. Sew through all the layers, anchoring your band in place. Loop the tab over to find the placement for your button. Attach the button with help from the buttons feature on page 106.

Pro Tip
If you're not really satisfied with the way the topstitching turned out on the front of your towel, cover it in ribbon! Use wide ribbon that covers your stitches and loop it around the back as you stitch it to the front.

All Zipped Up: Zippers

Many sewers, beginners, and frequent hobbyists alike, are deathly afraid of zippers. But I want you to know that you need not fear zippers any longer! With this foolproof method, you can be sure to master zippers and unlock a whole world of possibilities.

Varieties of zippers: Zippers can range from lightweight to heavyweight varieties. Thin coil is the lightweight option, perfect for small projects or light garments like skirts and dresses. Molded plastic is a middle-weight option, suited to jackets and heavy bags. Metal is a heavyweight option, often seen in jeans and heavy jackets. You'll see separating zippers, which are for jackets or other projects that need the zipper to separate, and also invisible zippers, which are designed for formal dresses.

Thin coil zippers are the easiest to work with and are used for the projects in this book. For the best results,

stick with them, as other zippers require more practice or different techniques. Be sure to get a zipper that's the required length mentioned in the materials list, or longer. You can always shorten a zipper, but you can't lengthen one. This method of applying zippers is called the centered zipper method.

Zipper feet: Zipper feet are a special attachment that may or may not have come with your machine. They replace the regular presser foot with something that looks a bit like a half foot. When you butt the zipper foot against the edge of your zipper, it allows you to sew as close as possible to the zipper without touching the teeth. Zipper feet aren't required to install the zippers here, but they do help.

Zipper feet: If your machine came with a zipper foot, it might look something like this—sort of a half-sized foot that lets you get very close to the zipper teeth.

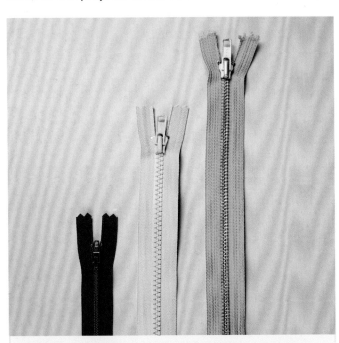

Varieties of zippers: You'll find coil, plastic, and metal varieties in the store, but coil zippers are by far the easiest to work with.

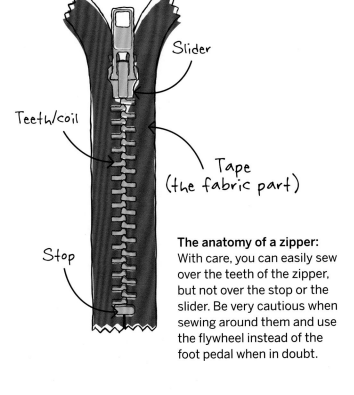

Slider

Teeth/coil

Tape (the fabric part)

Stop

The anatomy of a zipper: With care, you can easily sew over the teeth of the zipper, but not over the stop or the slider. Be very cautious when sewing around them and use the flywheel instead of the foot pedal when in doubt.

1 **Apply interfacing.** If you're working with a flimsy or even slightly stretchy fabric, fuse strips of 1" (2.5cm)-wide interfacing along the edges of your fabric pieces on the wrong side. This will keep your fabric from warping while you apply the zipper.

2 **Sew a straight seam.** If your project will not have a lining, be sure to finish the edges of your fabric before sewing this seam. Using a basting stitch, sew the two fabric pieces together with right sides facing, using a regular seam allowance. Press the seam fully open.

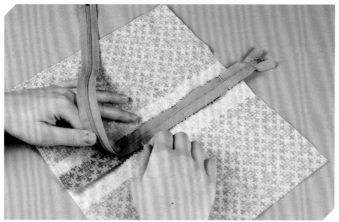

3 **Place the zipper.** Place your zipper face down on the wrong side of the seam you've created. With the projects in this book, it's fine if the beginning and end of the zipper run off the edges of the fabric. You can hold the zipper in place with pins, but scotch tape, a glue stick, or fusible web tape also work perfectly. No matter what, make sure the zipper teeth run perfectly straight down the center of the seam.

4 **Sew the zipper.** Switch to your zipper foot (if you have one) and, using a regular-length stitch, sew along one side, close to the edge of the zipper teeth. If you are making a project that has the zipper stop halfway down the fabric, you'll want to pivot your fabric and use the flywheel to slowly stitch over the zipper at the bottom end. Don't do this quickly or you could break your needle. Sew the other side of the zipper as you did the first.

5 **Remove the stitches.** Using your seam ripper, go back to the right side of your fabric and remove the stitches from the center seam. This should go smoothly because of the long stitch length. When you are finished, your zipper installation is complete, and the zipper is almost completely hidden within the seam!

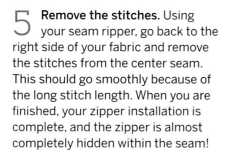

TRY YOUR ZIPPER-INSTALLING SKILLS:
Quick Zip Pouch

★ ★ ★ ☆ ☆ ☆ ☆

ESTIMATED TIME:
30–60 minutes

TECHNIQUES:
Zippers (page 114),
Finishing Seams (page 52),
Appliqué (page 64)

MAKES:
One 10" x 5" (20.5 x
12.5cm) pouch

Try out your zippering skills with this super easy pouch. It's the perfect size for pencils, makeup, or anything else. Plus, it comes together so quickly you'll want to make dozens. With the included octopus, argyle, and music note appliqué, each one will be different and exciting!

Materials

☐ ¼ yd. (25cm) of lightweight woven fabric

☐ One 12" (30.5cm) zipper

☐ Fat quarter or 6" x 6" (15 x 15cm) scrap of appliqué fabric (optional)

☐ 6" x 6" (15 x 15cm) square of fusible web (optional)

Tools

☐ Basic sewing kit (see page 28)

Your collection of fabric pieces for this project should look something like this:

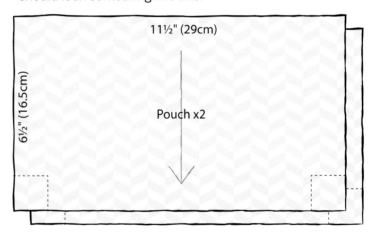

11½" (29cm)

6½" (16.5cm)

Pouch x2

THE PREP WORK:
Cut your fabric pieces using the following chart, and any appliqué pieces using the patterns on page 125.

Zippered Pouch Pieces

Piece Name	Material to Cut	Size to Cut	Number to Cut	Seam Allowance
Pouch	Lightweight woven	11½" x 6½"(29 x 16.5cm)	2	⅝" (1.5cm)
Appliqué design (optional)	Appliqué fabric and fusible web	To fit design	1	None

TRY YOUR ZIPPER-INSTALLING SKILLS:

Quick Zip Pouch (continued)

1 **Trim the corners.** Cut a 1" (2.5cm) square from each bottom corner of the pouch pieces (at each end of one of the long edges).

2 **Appliqué your design (optional).** See the appliqué feature on page 64 to choose a method for applying your decorative fabric to the pouch. Sew your appliqué pieces at least 2" (5cm) in from the sides or bottom of the pouch for the proper placement, sewing them on the right side of the fabric.

3 **Apply the zipper.** Following the steps in the zipper feature (page 114), apply the zipper along the top edge of the pouch pieces.

4 **Sew the sides and bottom.** Fold the pouch pieces in half along the zipper with right sides together. Move the zipper slider to the middle of the zipper and line up the side and bottom edges. Sew along these edges, going carefully over the zipper teeth and skipping over the corners. Iron and finish the seams.

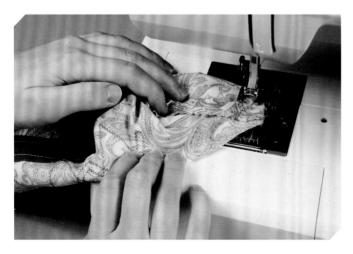

5 **Sew the corners.** Fold the pouch diagonally to make the side and bottom seams match up. Sew along this edge. Finish the seams.

High Class with a Hammer: Grommets & Eyelets

Grommets and eyelets are the kind of metal rings you see on your shoes, a curtain, or even some high-end purses. With just a little bit of practice, you can add these to your projects for a very professional look. Both grommets and eyelets serve to reinforce holes in fabric, allowing you to loop things through the hole, like handles or cording. Grommets typically refer to larger rings that are utilitarian, while eyelets are smaller and usually used on garments for decorative purposes.

Grommets: Because grommets are utilitarian, they generally only vary in finish and size. You can find them in brass or nickel typically, and they come in diameters of ½" (1.5cm) up to several inches wide. When shopping for your first grommets, be sure to get a kit, which should come with the grommet setting tool along with the grommets.

Varieties of grommets & eyelets: Because grommets are utilitarian, they don't often come in many varieties, but eyelets are more decorative, so lots of colors and finishes are available.

Eyelets: Because eyelets are more decorative than grommets, they tend to come in more colors. While you might only find brass and nickel in the notions section, check out the scrapbooking section, which sometimes has a large variety of eyelets that are used to decorate paper—but they can be used to decorate fabric as well! When buying your first eyelets, be sure to get a kit—this can include a small metal tool for hammering the eyelets, or a large hand-powered tool for squeezing them in place. I've had more luck with the hammering tool, so I suggest it highly. It's also less expensive.

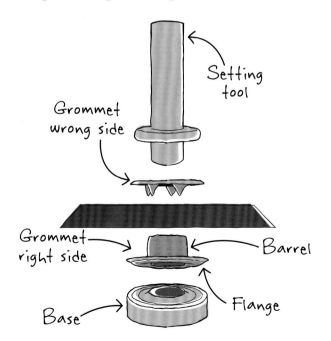

Anatomy of a grommet: A grommet is a two-piece item that sandwiches the fabric in between, securing the hole in the fabric so nothing frays or comes loose. It's important that a grommet is assembled in the correct order for a perfect fit.

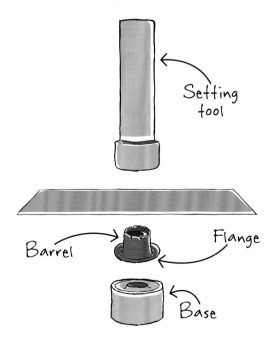

Anatomy of an eyelet: An eyelet is a one-piece system that has the barrel flare out to cover the hole in the fabric. It's important that it's hammered in the correct position for a perfect fit.

Installing grommets & eyelets: To install either a grommet or an eyelet in your fabric, follow these steps.

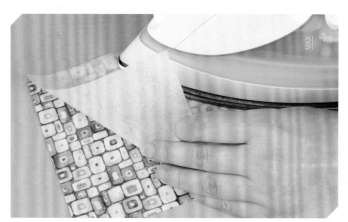

1 **Apply interfacing.** If you're working with lightweight fabric or just one layer of fabric, chances are your fabric will need some reinforcement to handle the grommets. Apply a strip or square of interfacing to the wrong side of the fabric to cover the area that will have a grommet.

2 **Cut a hole in the fabric.** Mark where your grommet will be placed and, using your seam ripper or a pair of tiny sharp scissors, cut a small hole through the layers of fabric. Check the fit by pushing your grommet/eyelet through the hole and keep gradually cutting it bigger until the fit is snug. If your grommet is particularly big, trim away the excess fabric to make a clean circular hole.

3 **For grommets: Place the grommet pieces.** A grommet typically comes as a two-piece system. Insert the right side of the grommet inward from the right side of your fabric and rest it upon the base of the setting tool. Nestle the wrong side of the grommet on top.

4 **For eyelets: Place the eyelet pieces.** Eyelets are only a one-piece system, as the barrel folds backward when it is struck to cover the fabric. Insert the barrel of the eyelet through the hole from the right side of your fabric. Rest the flange of the eyelet on the base of the setting tool.

5 **Hammer the grommet/eyelet.** Nestle the setting tool on the barrel of the grommet/eyelet and begin to hammer the top. The barrel of the grommet or eyelet should flatten and curl around the fabric beneath it, securing the piece in place. Pull at it when you are finished to make sure it's secure. If not, try hammering some more. But if something was placed incorrectly you'll have to pry the grommet/eyelet out and try again with a new piece.

Convenient Coin Pouch

★ ★ ★

ESTIMATED TIME:
15–30 minutes

TECHNIQUES:
Zippers (page 114),
Finishing Seams (page 52),
Grommets (page 119),
Sewing Curves (page 70)

MAKES:
One 3¾" x 3¾" (9.5 x 9.5cm) pouch

Try out your grommeting skills with this handy coin pouch. The grommet on the side makes it perfect for attaching it to your keys, purse, or backpack. It's great for spare change, but I like to use mine for aspirin for surprise headaches.

Materials

- ☐ ¼ yd. (25cm) of lightweight to medium-weight woven fabric
- ☐ One 8" (20.5cm)-long zipper
- ☐ One 1" (2.5cm) grommet
- ☐ Key ring or lanyard (optional)

Tools

- ☐ Basic sewing kit (see page 28)
- ☐ Grommet setting tools

Your collection of fabric pieces for this project should look something like this:

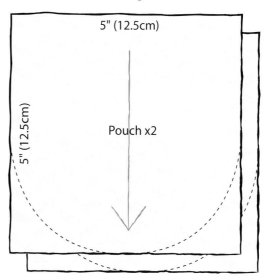

5" (12.5cm)

5" (12.5cm)

Pouch x2

THE PREP WORK:

Cut your fabric pieces using the following chart:

Coin Pouch Pieces

Piece Name	Material to Cut	Size to Cut	Number to Cut	Seam Allowance
Pouch	Light- to medium-weight woven	5" x 5"(12.5 x 12.5cm)	2	⅝" (1.5cm)

TRY YOUR GROMMETING SKILLS:

Convenient Coin Pouch (continued)

1 **Trim the pouch.** Align the two pouch pieces along the edges. Use a soup can, cup, or other round object to trace a rounded edge for your pouch. Trim the excess fabric away from both pieces of fabric so they are identical.

2 **Apply the zipper.** Following the steps in the zippers feature (page 114), apply the zipper along the top straight edge of the pouch pieces.

3 **Sew the sides.** Fold the pouch pieces in half along the zipper with right sides together. Move the zipper slide to the middle of the zipper and line up the edges. Sew along these edges, going carefully over the zipper teeth. Finish the seams, notch the seam allowances, turn the pouch right side out, and press the seams.

4 **Install the grommet.** Following the grommets feature (page 119), install a grommet in one of the upper corners of the pouch, going through all the fabric layers. Loop a key ring or lanyard through the pouch as desired.

In-a-Snap Wallet

pages 102–105

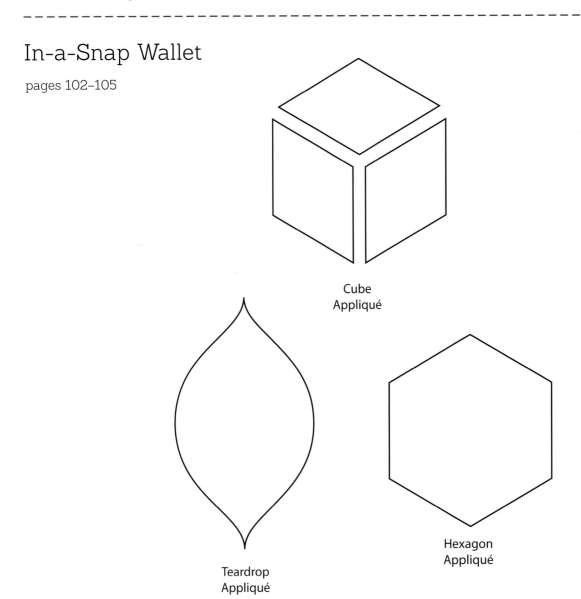

Cube
Appliqué

Teardrop
Appliqué

Hexagon
Appliqué

Patterns appear at actual size.

Quick Zip Pouch

pages 116–118

Argyle
Appliqué

Octopus
Appliqué

Music Notes
Appliqué

Patterns appear at actual size.

4

Easy Wearable Accessories

This chapter will help introduce you to the world of garments by starting with wearable accessories. If you're daunted by the idea of making clothes, this is a perfect way to get started without the hassle of fitting and adjusting. Just like with handmade garments, you'll be taking measurements of yourself to make accessories that fit just right, warming you up for making apparel that fits other major parts of your body later. With some quick measurements and easy techniques, you'll be making wrist cuffs, a scarf, and even an adorable hat! Best of all, these patterns are made entirely from body measurements, so that means you can use them to make clothes that fit the largest of friends to the littlest kids!

Skills to Master

☐ Taking Body Measurements

☐ Elastic

☐ Sewing Knit Fabrics

130 Radical Wrist Cuff

134 Snuggly Ruffled Scarf

139 Kitty Hat

Head to Toe: Taking Body Measurements

If you want to get into garment making, you'll need to know how to take accurate measurements. Luckily, knowing just a few basic measurements will get you very far. Using these basic measurements will aid you in selecting and cutting commercial patterns if you can see making more clothing in your future.

You can do most of these measurements with just your handy measuring tape. If you have trouble, you might find that you'll need a friend's help taking the measurements. Make sure that you measure while wearing the undergarments you plan to wear with the finished product, or at least a body-hugging leotard of some kind. Most important, make sure to be honest about the measurements.

While holding the tape, be sure not to squeeze or put any other undue stress on the body, just hold the tape until it feels snug. It helps to have a full-length mirror to make sure you are sitting up straight and holding the tape accurately.

Bust: This measurement is for the accurate fit of tops. Run the tape measure around the widest part of your chest area, making sure the tape is parallel to the floor.

Waist: This measurement is for the accurate fit of tops, dresses, and pants. Run the tape measure around the narrowest part of your torso, typically a few inches above your belly button. Make sure the tape is parallel to the floor.

Low waist: This measurement is for the accurate fit of pants. Run the tape measure around the area where you usually wear your pants, typically between the belly button and hips. Make sure the tape is parallel to the floor.

Hips: This measurement is for the accurate fit of pants and dresses. Run the tape measure around the widest part of the torso, usually about 7"–9" (18–23cm) beneath the waist line. Make sure the tape is parallel to the floor.

Back length: This measurement is for the length of tops and dresses. Begin the tape measure at the first neck bone—this is the topmost vertebra that protrudes from between the shoulders. Run the tape down to where you want your project to end, such as at the low waist for tops and at the knees for dresses.

Arm: This measurement is for the accurate fit of sleeves. Begin the tape measure at the top of the shoulder bone. You should feel the bone protruding in the area above your shoulder muscle. Run the tape down your arm to where you want your sleeve to end, such as at the wrist bone for long sleeves.

Knowing these measurements will allow you to pick out just the right size clothing pattern, as commercial patterns are usually dependent on the major three sizes: bust, waist, and hips. The additional measurements can be used to check against your pattern pieces if you are especially short or tall.

In commercial patterns, each of your measurements will have additional length added to it, not only for seam allowances, but also for ease. This is the sewing term used to describe the extra size given to a garment so a person is free to move around in it. It is essentially what determines the garment's bagginess. A large amount of ease will mean the clothing is free-flowing and loose, while a small amount of ease means it will fit closely.

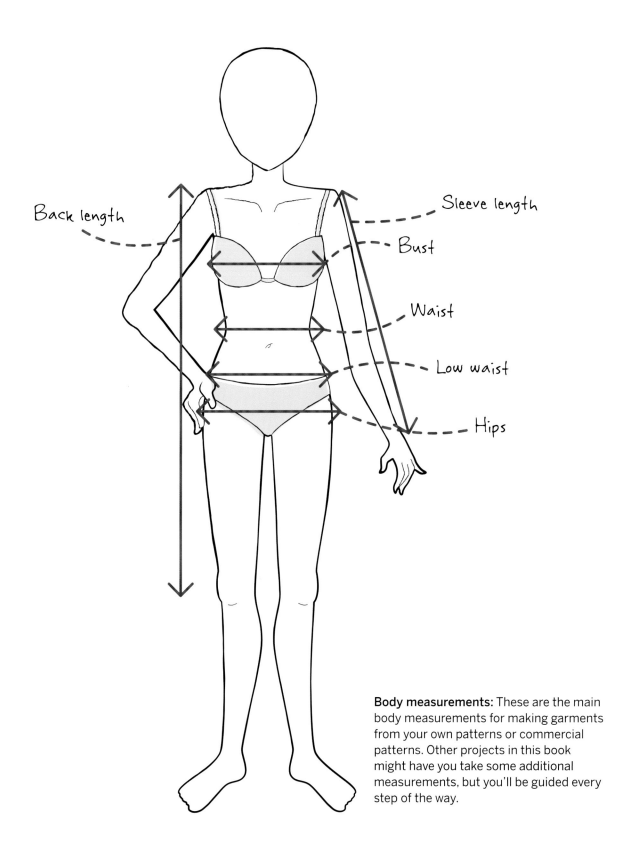

Back length

Sleeve length

Bust

Waist

Low waist

Hips

Body measurements: These are the main body measurements for making garments from your own patterns or commercial patterns. Other projects in this book might have you take some additional measurements, but you'll be guided every step of the way.

TRY YOUR MEASURING SKILLS:
Radical Wrist Cuff

★ ★ ☆ ☆ ☆ ☆ ☆ ☆

🕐	**ESTIMATED TIME:**	30–60 minutes
	TECHNIQUES:	Snaps (page 100), Body Measurements (page 128), Interfacing (page 80)
✓	**MAKES:**	One 2½" (6.5cm)-wide cuff sized to fit your wrist

Test your body measuring skills with this adorable cuff. Appliqué it with your choice of Japanese writing, a star, or a skull, and it will easily replace your favorite bracelet!

Materials

- ☐ ⅛ yd. (12.5cm) of light- to medium-weight woven fabric
- ☐ ⅛ yd. (12.5cm) of lightweight fusible interfacing
- ☐ Three sew-in or two metal prong snaps, no more than ½" (1.5cm) wide
- ☐ Fat quarter or 3" x 3" (7.5 x 7.5cm) scrap of appliqué fabric (optional)
- ☐ 3" x 3" (7.5 x 7.5cm) square of fusible web (optional)

Tools

- ☐ Basic sewing kit (see page 28)
- ☐ Chopstick or similar turning tool

MEASUREMENTS

Work out this equation to find out what size pieces to cut. Feel free to round up to the nearest ¼" or 0.5cm for each final measurement to make things easier.

Wrist circumference + 4" (10cm) = _____ A (wrist cuff length)

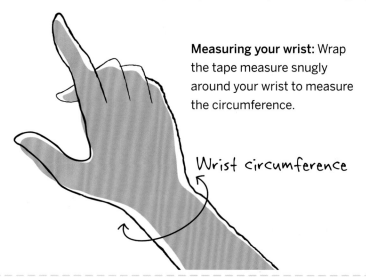

Measuring your wrist: Wrap the tape measure snugly around your wrist to measure the circumference.

Wrist circumference

THE PREP WORK:

Cut your fabric pieces using the following chart, and any appliqué pieces using the patterns on page 142.

Wrist Cuff Pieces

Piece Name	Material to Cut	Size to Cut	Number to Cut	Seam Allowance
Cuff	Light- to medium-weight woven	A x 3¾" (A x 9.5cm)	2	⅝" (1.5cm)
Interfacing	Lightweight interfacing	A x 3¾" (A x 9.5cm)	1	⅝" (1.5cm)
Appliqué design (optional)	Appliqué fabric and fusible web	To fit design	1	None

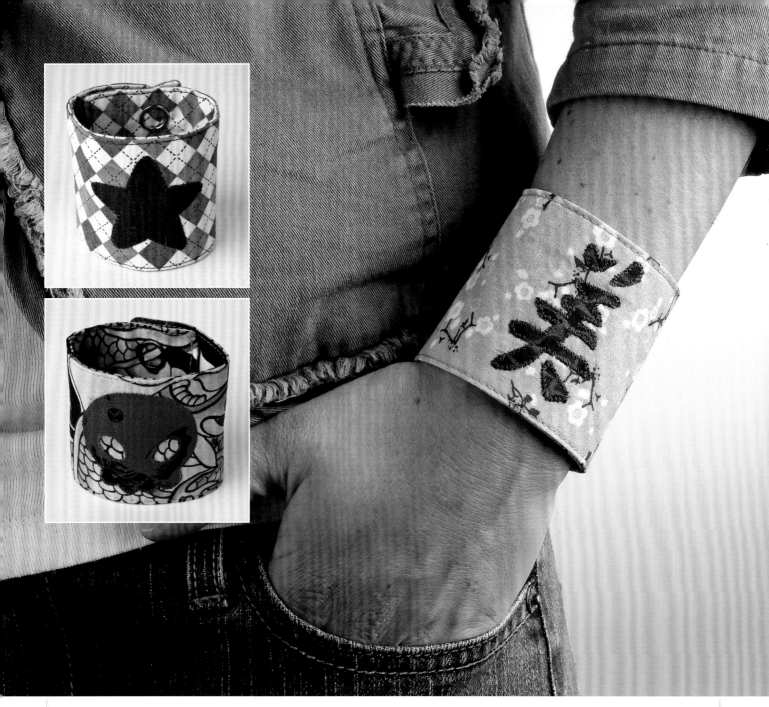

Your collection of fabric pieces for this project should look something like this:

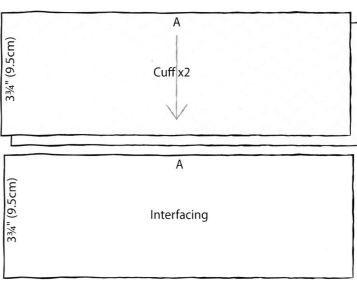

3¾" (9.5cm)

A

Cuff x2

3¾" (9.5cm)

A

Interfacing

TRY YOUR MEASURING SKILLS:

Radical Wrist Cuff (continued)

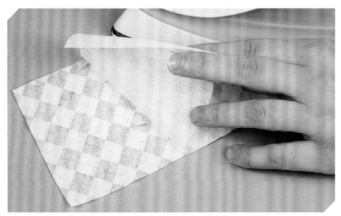

1 **Apply the interfacing.** Select the piece of fabric you want to use for the top of your cuff. Line up the interfacing over this fabric piece. Following the manufacturer's directions, fuse it to the wrong side of the fabric completely.

2 **Appliqué your design (optional).** See the appliqué feature on page 64 to choose a method for applying your decorative fabric to the right side of the cuff piece with the interfacing attached. Sew your appliqué on the center of the cuff or at least 1" (2.5cm) from the edge of the fabric.

3 **Sew the cuff.** Lay your cuff pieces right sides together and mark a 5" (12.5cm) line along the bottom long edge of the cuff. This marks your opening for turning. Sew around the entire cuff, skipping over the line. Trim the seam allowances, turn the cuff right side out, and press it flat.

4 **Edge stitch the cuff.** Tuck in the seam allowances around the opening and press them flat. Edge stitch around the perimeter of the cuff, about ⅛" (0.5cm) from the outside seam. Doing this should close up the opening.

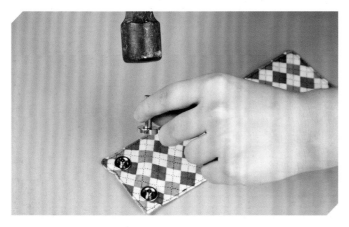

5 **Install the snaps.** Install the stud half of two or three snaps on the back side of the cuff along one of the short edges. Install the studs so they will face downward when the cuff is closed. See the snaps feature (page 100) for more help. Try on the cuff and mark where the snap sockets should be installed. Install them on the top side of the cuff at the opposite edge. Install the sockets so they will face upward when the cuff is closed.

Stretched into Shape: Elastic

Nearly everyone has heard of elastic. It's the stretchy stuff that comes in bands and makes your clothes snug and fit well. When sewing with clothing patterns, there's no need to worry about whether the clothes are too loose or too tight. With the right size of elastic, the clothes will stretch to accommodate any size.

Varieties: Elastic can be separated into two categories: utilitarian and decorative. Utilitarian elastic is usually not seen in the finished garment. It comes in strips that can be as wide as several inches and is undeniably strong. This elastic stretches a great deal with little pulling and has great lasting power. It usually only comes in basic black and white, though a few colorful varieties are available for projects where the elastic can be seen on the outside.

Decorative elastic is not as strong or long lasting as other elastics, but it looks much prettier and is often used on the outside of garments. You'll usually find this elastic on lingerie and decorative tops. For that reason, these elastics are better suited to more experienced sewers and we won't be using them here.

Elastic is typically used so you can stretch your clothes to easily put them on and move around in them. At the same time, it's used to hold your clothes in place while you're wearing them. Elastic strips are cut close to your body measurement so while at rest they fit comfortably and while putting clothes on they stretch to fit. The simplest method of applying elastic is to create a casing for it. A double-fold hem is made and the elastic is guided through it with a safety pin.

Elastic can be used to create waistbands or as a decorative element on your projects. It can also be used to quickly create gathers in fabric, as is done with the Snuggly Ruffled Scarf project (page 134).

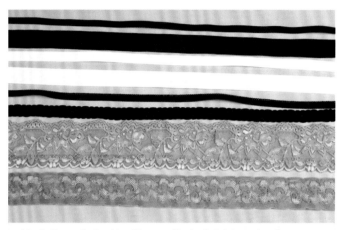

Varieties of elastic: Strong (but plain) bands of elastic are primarily used for their tough and stretchy qualities, while lacey decorative elastic is more delicate and cannot stand up to as much pulling.

TRY YOUR ELASTIC-INSTALLING SKILLS:
Snuggly Ruffled Scarf

★ ★ ★ ☆ ☆ ☆ ☆ ☆

🕐 **ESTIMATED TIME:**
30–60 minutes

TECHNIQUES:
Elastic (page 133)

✓ **MAKES:**
One 7½" x 20"–30"
(19 x 51–76cm) scarf

Test your skills at using elastic with this cozy scarf. The elastic works its magic by ruffling up the scarf with no gathering required!

Materials

- ☐ ½ yd. (50cm) of lightweight woven fabric, 45" (114.5cm) wide for a collar-length scarf, 60" (152.5cm) wide for a longer scarf
- ☐ ⅜" (1cm)-wide elastic, 20" (51cm) long for a collar-length scarf, 30" (76cm) long for a longer scarf

Tools

- ☐ Basic sewing kit (see page 28)
- ☐ Safety pin
- ☐ Chopstick or similar turning tool

Your collection of fabric pieces for this project should look something like this:

```
        44" (112cm) or 58" (147.5cm)
8¾" (22cm)
        Scarf x2
```

THE PREP WORK:
Cut your fabric pieces using the following chart:

Scarf Pieces

Piece Name	Material to Cut	Size to Cut	Number to Cut	Seam Allowance
Collar-length Scarf	Lightweight woven	8¾" x 44" (22 x 112cm)	2	⅝" (1.5cm)
Long Scarf	Lightweight woven	8¾" x 58" (22 x 147.5cm)	2	⅝" (1.5cm)

TRY YOUR ELASTIC-INSTALLING SKILLS:

Snuggly Ruffled Scarf (continued)

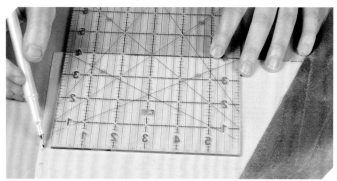

1 **Mark the openings.** On the wrong side of the fabric, make a mark 4⅛" (10.5cm) in from the edge on the short ends of the scarf. Repeat this for the opposite edge on the same end. This should leave a ½" (1.5cm) space in the center of that end. This marks the opening for your elastic. Repeat on the other short end. Mark a 5" (12.5cm) line centered along the edge of one of the long sides. This marks your opening for turning right side out.

2 **Sew the scarf perimeter.** Line up the raw edges of the scarf pieces with right sides facing and sew completely around the perimeter, skipping over the elastic openings and turning opening. Trim the seam allowances, turn the fabric right side out, define the corners with a chopstick, and press the seams. Go back and use a hand-sewn ladder stitch to sew the opening in the side of the scarf closed.

3 **Sew the channel.** Draw a line 3½" (9cm) in from one long side of the scarf. Make sure the line is parallel to the opening for your elastic and goes the entire length of the scarf. Repeat this along the other long side. Sew along these lines to create the channel for your elastic.

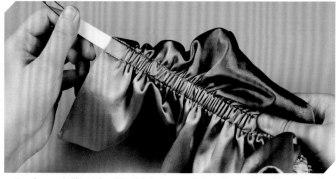

4 **Insert the elastic.** Using a safety pin, guide the elastic through the channel sewn in the center of your scarf. Once the opposite end of the elastic enters the casing and is just barely covered, anchor that end down by stitching over it several times. Continue guiding the elastic through the casing as the fabric gathers. When you reach the opposite end, anchor that end of elastic the same way you did the first end.

5 **Anchor the elastic.** Adjust the fabric so the gathers are even. Set your stitch to a slightly longer length and prepare to sew through the elastic. Starting at the top, grab a 5" (12.5cm) or so section on your scarf and stretch out your elastic as far as it will go. Sew through the stretched elastic until you reach your fingers, then repeat the process until you reach the end of your scarf.

Tip
This project is a great excuse to try out flimsy fabrics like lightweight satin. It works perfectly for this pattern and makes a very dressy accessory!

Stretch Savvy: Sewing Knit Fabrics

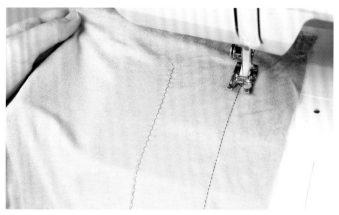

Stretch stitches: A narrow zigzag stitch or machine stretch stitch will allow your seams to stretch along with your knit fabrics.

Once you've gotten a handle on sewing with different weights and textures of woven fabrics, why not try out knits? They can be a little unpredictable at times, and that's why it helps to have some background knowledge about fabrics so you can be ready for anything unexpected the knits might throw at you.

Varieties of knits: As mentioned in the fabrics section (page 18), there are large varieties of light- and medium-weight knits to choose from. Medium-weight knits typically stretch less than lightweight knits and are therefore easier to sew. Start with the thicker varieties before working your way down to slinkier fabrics.

Knit grain lines: Hopefully you've been keeping to your grain line when you cut your fabric from wovens, but if not, it's very important to do so with knits. Because knits stretch across the horizontal grain (and sometimes also the vertical grain), it's crucial that the pattern pieces line up to go along with this stretch. A t-shirt wouldn't fit as well if it only stretched up and down and didn't stretch around your body, would it? So think one step ahead if you can and imagine where the fabric needs to stretch when you cut it.

Cutting knits: Some lightweight knits can be slinky and move in unpredictable ways while you cut them. A good way to tame these fabrics is to lay them on tissue paper (or newspaper if you don't mind washing off ink) before you cut them. As you pin your pieces and cut them, make sure you go through all the layers. Try to downgrade to your craft scissors for this if possible, as the tissue paper can dull your sewing shears.

Sewing needle for knits: As mentioned in the getting started section, there are special sewing machine needles designed for knit fabrics. They have a rounded tip that allows the needle to punch between threads rather than right through. If your seams aren't turning out how you'd like, check to be sure that you're using a sewing needle for knits.

Stretch stitches: Because your finished garment will be stretchy, your seams should stretch along with it or the threads might break. If your machine has a stretch stitch, then you're in business! It will often use a kind of two-steps-forward, one-step-back motion that works to give the garment some stretch. If your machine doesn't have a stretch stitch, a zigzag stitch with a narrow width and medium length is a great substitute.

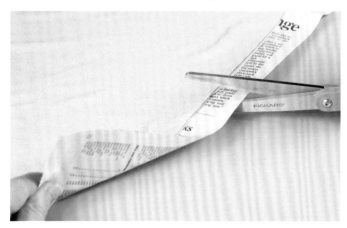

Cutting knits: Cut your knit fabrics with a layer of tissue or newspaper underneath for more stability, but be sure to use craft scissors if you can.

The problem with knits: The main issue with knits is how they tend to stretch while you sew them. No matter how little you touch the fabric, the pressure of the presser foot and the pulling of the needle seem to do something that gives you warped, wavy seams—especially at the hems. However, once you finally get things working in your favor and your seams are perfectly flat and neat, knits are joy to work with! Your seams will look much more fluid and smooth, your garments will fit you comfortably and perfectly, and you don't have to worry about finished seams! Knits don't unravel, so putting together knit projects is super quick! Here are some tips for keeping your knits from stretching out of shape while you sew:

Hands off: Even if you might not realize it, you could be pushing or pulling at your fabric while you sew. Try to consciously put less pressure on the fabric while you guide it and your seams might turn out better.

Ease the presser foot: If your machine has an adjustable presser control for the presser foot, bring it down to the lowest pressure (but not 0). The presser foot won't push down as much on the fabric, causing it to stretch.

Easing: Easing is a technique usually used for woven fabrics to give the fabric a light, even, and almost unnoticeable distribution of gathers along an edge. In knit fabrics, this works to prevent stretched stitches and puckers. While you sew your seam, press down behind the fabric so the fabric feeding through the machine begins to build up. Your sewing will start to slow down, and when it slows to almost no motion, let the fabric go and press your finger down again.

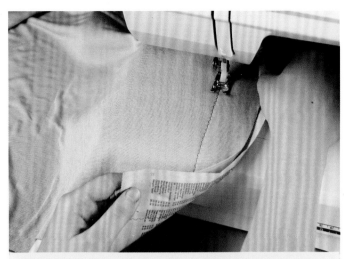

Stabilizing your stitches: As a trump card, layering tissue or newspaper beneath your fabric will stop any stretching dead in its tracks. Just be careful when tearing away the paper afterward.

Stabilizing: If your knits are still giving you trouble, especially if they are thin enough that the needle forces them down through the throat plate, stabilizer is a very reliable solution. Use tissue paper, newspaper, or very lightweight stabilizer beneath your fabric as you sew. When you finish, gently tear the paper away from your stitches to avoid breaking them.

Ironing: Even if your stitches seem a little wobbly after you sew, try giving them an iron to see if they smooth out. In a lot of cases they will improve quite a bit, so there's no need to worry about how your seams look right out of the machine.

Easing: This is a subtle technique that creates light gathers in your fabric, effectively canceling out the stretching that might happen while you sew knits.

Kitty Hat

★ ★ ☆ ☆ ☆

ESTIMATED TIME:
20–40 minutes

TECHNIQUES:
Sewing Knits (page 137),
Appliqué (page 64),
Hemming (page 53),
Body Measurements (page 128)

MAKES:
One hat sized to fit your head

Materials

☐ ⅓ yd. (33cm) of fleece fabric

☐ Fat quarter or 6" x 6" (15 x 15cm) scrap of appliqué fabric (optional)

☐ 6" x 6" (15 x 15cm) square of fusible web (optional)

Tools

☐ Basic sewing kit (see page 28)

Try out your knit-sewing skills with this warm and adorable fleece hat. Fleece is a perfect knit for beginners and sews very easily. You'll be surprised that this hat is only two squares! The corners of the squares make cute kitty ear shapes that really go with the added appliqué face choices.

MEASUREMENTS

Work out these equations to find out what size pieces to cut. Feel free to round up to the nearest ¼" or 0.5cm for each final measurement to make things easier.

Head circumference ÷ 2 + 1¼" (3cm) = _____ A (Hat width)

Head top* ÷ 2 + 1¼" (3cm) = _____ B (Hat depth)

*Measure from where you want your hat to begin in front of your face to where you want it to end behind your head. This measurement can differ depending on your size and preferences, but an average adult is about 15" (38cm).

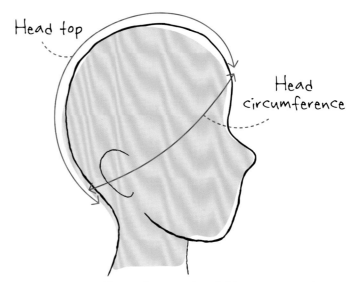

Measuring your head: Measure around your head and from front to back to determine the size of your hat.

Kitty Hat (continued)

Your collection of fabric pieces for this project should look something like this:

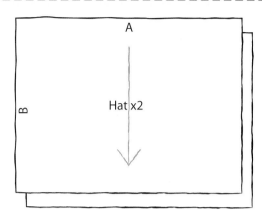

THE PREP WORK:

Cut your fabric pieces using the following chart, and any appliqué pieces using the patterns on page 142.

Kitty Hat Pieces

Piece Name	Material to Cut	Size to Cut	Number to Cut	Seam Allowance
Hat front & back	Fleece	A x B	2	⅝" (1.5cm)
Appliqué design (optional)	Appliqué fabric and fusible web	To fit design	1	None

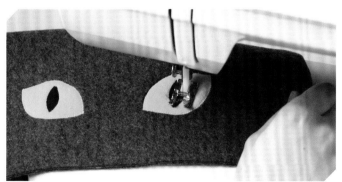

1 **Appliqué your design (optional).** See the appliqué feature on page 64 to choose a method for applying your decorative fabric to the hat. Sew your appliqué on the right side of one of your hat pieces, centering it vertically or placing it at least 1½" (4cm) up from the bottom edge. This piece will be the front of your hat.

2 **Sew the sides.** Line up the front and back hat pieces with right sides together. Sew along the sides and top, leaving the bottom edge free for turning right side out. Trim the seam allowances, press the seams, and turn right side out.

3 **Hem the bottom.** Fold under the bottom edge toward the wrong side by ⅝" (1.5cm) and press the fold in place. Sew along this edge to create a single-fold hem.

Radical Wrist Cuff

pages 130–132

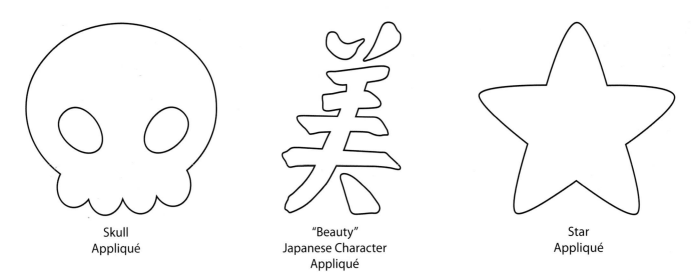

Skull
Appliqué

"Beauty"
Japanese Character
Appliqué

Star
Appliqué

Radical Wrist Cuff patterns appear at actual size.

Kitty Hat

pages 139–141

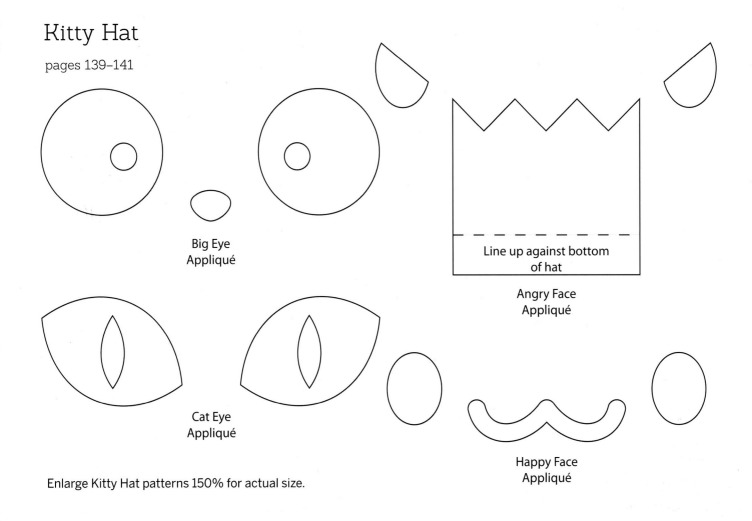

Big Eye
Appliqué

Line up against bottom
of hat

Angry Face
Appliqué

Cat Eye
Appliqué

Happy Face
Appliqué

Enlarge Kitty Hat patterns 150% for actual size.

Index

Note: Page numbers in *italics* indicate projects/patterns.

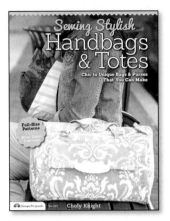

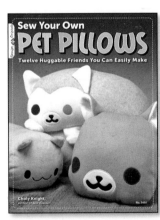

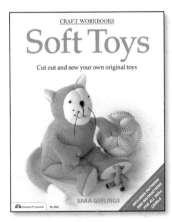
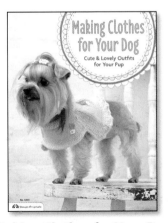
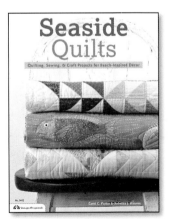